INCIDENTAL MUSIC

Remarkable Stories about the World's Greatest Composers

DAVID OTT

CONTENTS

I. Incident at the Monastery at Pomposa

Abbot Antonio was the head priest of the monastery. As he finished his morning prayers, he rose from his knees to see his young assistant fidgeting anxiously.

"What is it?" asked Antonio.

"There is a messenger to see you. He is from Rome. The Holy Father sent him directly." This prompted his full attention.

"Send him in immediately," directed Antonio.

The courier entered the chambers and delivered his message. Antonio listened intently. He took in every word with interest. The news came as a shock to him.

"That is the message? You are sure of every word?" Antonio asked.

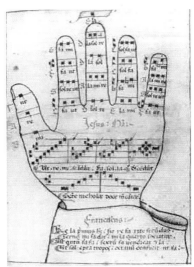

Guidonian Hand

The messenger assured him, "As God is my witness." The words were spoken like an oath. Antonio dismissed the messenger, but the words were still ringing in his ears. Now the room was bathed in silence. Antonio was sure the news would cause quite a stir among the monks.

Antonio called his assistant. "Fetch Brothers Benedetto and Claudio." His assistant, Raphael, could feel the tension in his voice. The message from the Holy Father left Antonio with a dilemma. He had some convincing to do. Of the brotherhood of monks, these two, Benedetto and Claudio, would be the most difficult to convince.

"If I can change the hearts of these two, the others will follow." He spoke the words with a deep sense of hope.

Benedetto and Claudio arrived. Each was confused by the urgency of this calling.

Benedetto was the first to speak. "What is it?"

Claudio added, "We are here to serve you and God in any way."

Although they were ready to serve, Antonio was not sure they would enjoy the task he would be asking of them.

"I have news here that Guido, the master musician of the Order of St. Benedict, will be rejoining our monastery here at Pomposa. I will need your help."

Benedetto and Claudio were stunned. The news hit them like a bolt! "But Father Antonio, Guido is so..." He let the words fall without speaking them. The words he had intended were cruel, not worthy of a monk. "Well, he is so arrogant." There, he had spoken the word. "Father Antonio, arrogance is offensive in any person, particularly a monk of the Order of St. Benedict, as Guido is."

"That may be so, but the Holy Father, Pope John XIX himself, has directed us to accept him and his teachings."

"His teachings!" cried out Claudio. "It is bad enough to accept the man, but his teachings too. That is asking too much. When he was here earlier, he had the whole of the Brotherhood up in arms. We grew sick and tired of his corrections. His irksome suggestions. His 'rectifications' as he called them."

"Were they not helpful?" asked Father Antonio.

It was difficult for them to admit that Guido of Arezzo had good ideas. His teaching methods were effective. It was his air of superiority that disturbed the brothers.

Benedetto complained, "His concepts are so radical."

Claudio added, "It would take a great deal of time to implement such methods."

Antonio raised his hand, directing the palm at both of them. "Enough. I have heard enough. You are instructed to welcome him, in the courteous spirit of our monastery. You are to receive him graciously. You are *not* to speak unkindly about him with the brothers. Am I clear?"

They understood. But their reluctance could hardly go unnoticed.

Father Antonio put up his hands indicating he was not taking any more complaints. He simply directed them, "Then, go, and do as God would have you do."

Certainly Benedetto and Claudio had their reasons. For years Guido of Arezzo had been a thorn in the flesh. He was a man with his own theories about the teaching of music. His were revolutionary methods and most disturbing was his adamant insistence on their implementation. It was he and his agenda that caused the friction among the brothers.

No one could deny that there were problems. For several centuries the Catholic Church had insisted on new melodies for Holy Mass. By the 11th century, a great many chant melodies had been added to the usual services. In addition, demands for new music were created for sacred festivals. So many melodies had been created that it was nearly impossible to commit them to memory. That is where the problem existed. No system had been developed that accurately recorded the tunes.

Guido, like so many musicians of his day, had grown frustrated by the immense body of Gregorian Chant melodies that they were required to memorize. They had to be committed to memory because no satisfactory system of notation had been developed. The best any copyist could come up with was a squiggle or two that outlined the shape of the tune. These marks were placed more or less above a word of the text. Nothing was definite. Each doodle was hardly more than a suggestion. The system was inadequate and antiquated. Guido had some solution. However, his condescending attitude upset the brethren. Passions ran high against him.

As a choirmaster, Guido grew weary of his choir members who frequently failed to learn properly or sing the melodies accurately.

"Singers of the choir, why do you stumble over these melodies? These are sacred tunes given to us by Pope Gregory and others?"

"There are so many," complained one chorister after another. "How can we remember them all? Even the lines and squiggles above the words don't help much."

Guido agreed something had to be done in order to teach the chorus members how to learn and recall the hundreds of melodies sung in worship. A plan formulated in his mind. It began as Guido was singing through the *Hymn to St. John*. It was this melody that provided him with an important key to the teaching of singing. He believed it unlocked a secret he could use to teach his choirs to learn music quicker and how to sing more accurately. Once he had the key, he worked out the details.

Standing before the cantors, he announced he had uncovered a secret held in the *Hymn to St. John.* "It is a melody from two centuries ago," he announced. "The chant has a unique design. Each phrase begins on a pitch one step higher than the previous phrase. First, let's look at the text of the hymn. Of course the text is Latin, the pure language of the church."

"The words of the text read: '*Ut queant laxis,*' '*Resonare fibris,*' '*Mira gestorum,*' '*Famili tuorum,*' '*Solve polluti,*' '*Labii reatum.*'"

He told the choristers, "Each phrase begins on a pitch that is one step higher than the preceding phrase. "*Ut*" begins on the pitch C. "*Re,*" the first syllable of the word "*resonare,*" begins on D. "*Mi,*" the first syllable of the word "*Mira,*" begins on E. The pattern continues upward in the same manner. The first phrase begins on C, the second phrase D, the third phrase on E, then F, G and finally A. From this hymn, I have devised a plan to name each note of the scale. In order, they shall be: "ut re mi fa sol la." I created the name of each note from the first syllable of each phrase. Not only will the notes be given a name, but notice, too, how pure each vowel is for singing. "Re, mi, fa, sol, la" are open and clear. All the vowels are excellent for singing, though I admit, I find "ut" quite unsatisfactory. For this name, I have substituted "do" for the syllable "ut." "Do" is the first syllable of Domino, the Latin word for God. That serves two purposes, it is holy and it is a pure vowel for singing. Under this new system, the notes of the scale will be: "do, re, mi, fa, sol, la."

To teach the choristers to improve their singing skills, Guido explained that when he called a certain name, such as "mi" or "sol," the members were to sing that pitch. He told them this would give them something concrete to hold on to, given the fact that music is quite abstract.

Guido did not stop there. He sought to improve his plan. "Brothers, I have developed my idea even further. It would be awkward to call the name of each note, so I have created an illustration that will work as a shortcut. Instead of speaking the syllable, I shall point to a specific spot on my hand. Each part of my hand, the palm, the fingers and the joints will represent a pitch. When I point to a specific spot on my hand, you shall sing the pitch associated with that point. I have drawn the diagram of a hand with the representative names on it to illustrate my point."

The plan succeeded. The choir did improve. Guido wasn't through yet.

He told them, "Singing is so abstract. I have created a novel way for all singers to learn and recall the melodies with specificity. I have created a method to write and copy the melodies. It begins with a musical staff that consists of four parallel lines. Each line shall represent a pitch of music. The lowest line shall represent F. Two lines above that, shall represent C. With these two reference points, we shall have specificity. Composers of new melodies will be able to notate each note precisely."

In spite of their resentment against Guido, they began to understand his ideas. "Specific pitches representing an abstract art form?" pondered one brother. "It could be helpful."

Though his methods were bringing excellent results, resentment among the brethren was rising because of Guido's personality.

"He's a know-it-all," fumed Brother Guillaume.

"Bighead," replied Brother Pietro.

"I find his methods an insult to intelligence," remarked one chorister who intended to remain anonymous.

While his fellow monks dismayed of Guido and his ideas, Guido developed an ally. It was none other than Pope John XIX. By 1033, word of Guido's clever teaching methods reached the Holy See. Pope John found that Guido's ideas greatly facilitated his ability to learn and recall the melodies. He liked the results. He directed that a message be sent to Father Guido.

"Bring Guido of Arezzo to me," the Holy Father ordered. "I find his singing methods of great value to me personally. His ideas have improved my ability to learn melodies. Now I do so with ease. In the past I was required to use a master musician to teach me the melodies. Now I am able do so on my own. Guido's ideas are of great benefit. I want Guido here in Rome to instruct our clergy."

Guido accepted Pope John's request to settle in Rome. Unfortunately, the climate did not agree with him. He contracted Roman fever and had to return to the monastery at Pomposa, where climate conditions were more favorable to him.

After Guido had settled in, his Brothers took to him with more favor. One month after his return, Abbott Antonio called a meeting with Benedetto and Claudio. They met after the morning Matins service.

"It has been a month since Guido has returned from Rome to us. Brothers, what have you observed?"

Brother Claudio spoke first, his voice was filled with enthusiasm. "The Brothers now admire him."

Benedetto gleefully agreed. "The choir sings with confidence. The monks learn new chants with ease."

"But what about Brother Guido himself, have the Brethren accepted him?"

"They have. With open arms too."

"We are *delighted* to have him in our flock."

"And Guido, how does he feel about all this?"

"Quite at home, I believe," Benedetto pronounced.

Author's note: While Guido d'Arezzo was a real person. Abbot Antonio, and Brothers Benedetto, Claudio, Guillaume, Pietro and the assistant, Raphael, were fictitious.

II. Incident at Notre Dame

The year was 1163. Maurice de Sully, both a monk and a builder, knelt in the dirt. Resting his left arm on his left knee, he took the index finger of his right hand and began drawing in the dirt. His heart trembled with excitement as he pondered his great vision.

"This is the beginning," he told himself, "of a great and majestic building dedicated to the glory of God." His finger moved forward to the east. Then he stopped. For a moment, he took his attention away from the earth. He lifted his head and once again, there it was. The sight made him shudder. His eyes fell on the miserable sight before him. It was the church of Paris.

Cathedral of Notre Dame of Paris

"What a dismal statement that house of God is," his voice wrought with distain. "Here I am the Bishop of Paris. I sit in the greatest city of Europe. All the kings worship here, yet this church is a wretched excuse for a house of God." Looking more intently at the edifice before him, now in its dilapidated state, he pronounced it unfit for a church of such importance. He mumbled to himself, "It is a church unworthy of both God and man."

Maurice de Sully was the bishop of Paris, the greatest city of Europe in 1163. The population of Paris was reaching 200,000 people. It was a city of great breadth, larger than any other city of the day. Few cities were greater than 40,000. Paris was home to five times that amount. It was also home to the official church of kings from throughout Europe. Each traveled to worship at the Paris church.

Returning to his sketch in the dirt, he declared the old building too worn out to be repaired. Shaking his head, "It must come down," he ordered.

The bishop continued his sketch. He had determined that the outline of the great cathedral would be in the shape of the Latin cross. It was now customary in Europe to use the cross as the design of the exterior of a cathedral. The cross was the great symbol of Christianity.

Maurice was positioned on a large island of the Siene River facing east, near the southwest bank of the river. It was the place where the great cathedral would be built. In the earth, he outlined the shape of a cross. However, it included an arc at the top, rather than a flat line.

The image of a cross was clearly laid out before him. The long section would serve as the nave which would hold the parishioners who would come for Holy Mass. The two arms of the cross formed the transepts. These two areas would serve as chapels for small services or for places of worship for wealthy donors. Maurice even accounted for burial places for worthy saints or wealthy donors. He designated areas alongside the altar for the positioning of the choir.

Maurice began to hum a solemn melody. It was a reverent tune suitable for worship in the great cathedral he was proposing. Then he began to sing the words of the text.

"Lord have mercy. Christ have mercy. Lord have Mercy." He reminded himself of the beauty of both the music and the text. Quietly, he spoke to himself, "How meaningful and beautiful are the words of the Kyrie of the Mass."

Maurice recalled that the tune he was humming was hundreds of years old. It had probably been composed by Pope Gregory around the year 600. No one was positive that the melody had been written by Gregory himself. The church service was filled with a great many melodies attributed to him because he had been such a great lover of music. Pope Gregory had been a great champion of music within the Catholic Church. Not only had he composed melodies for worship, he collected all the melodies that were sung in the church. Then he organized them. He declared certain melodies to be appropriate for the various services of the day or of the church year. Some were brighter melodies suitable for festivals and holy days, while darker, more somber tunes, were best used for solemn services. As a whole, they became known as Gregorian chant melodies.

Understanding that music was a key component of worship, Pope Gregory ordered a school for singing to be created. It became known as the *Schola Cantorum*, the school for singing. It would be used to teach priests to learn the chants and how to sing properly.

Each singer was required to learn scores of melodies, commit them to memory, sing them to perfection, then pass them on to others, who in turn began the process all over again. Music passed from generation to generation. To help, lines and squiggles above the words were occasionally added to remind the singers of the flow of the melody, but everything had to be memorized first. Though he lived more than 400 years after

Pope Gregory, Guido d'Arezzo was the man who devised a musical staff of four lines. It proved successful and gave musicians a system to write and recall the melodies. Maurice was glad for Guido's clever inventions.

The Kyrie melody Maurice was humming brought him great comfort. "Comfort isn't what I need right now," he insisted. "I need to continue my vision." He focused his attention to the drawing on the ground. "Next, I must create an entrance that will be majestic. It must overpower." Then he added softly, "It must also appeal to the senses and emotions."

Now that Bishop Maurice had drawn a sketch of the great cathedral, it was time to approach several architects. Already by 1163, other great churches had been constructed. A few of the newer cathedrals were making use of the pointed arch. Great pillars of stone, standing twenty yards apart, soared up to a hundred feet into the air. They were joined at the top by a vaulted arch that formed a point at their convergence. Cathedrals from previous generations were joined by a rounded arch. The pointed arch offered architects greater freedom. Because the pointed arch distributed the immense weight of the building across a great area, architects could design walls that were spectacularly higher than before.

With walls built of stone that stood more than a hundred feet tall, their great weight caused a problem. When the roof was attached to the outer walls, the pressure forced the walls outward, causing them to collapse. It was necessary to give inward support in order to prevent a catastrophe. Buttresses, which were walls placed perpendicular to the cathedral walls, were added to give the necessary support. Half a dozen or so of these buttresses might line each side of the outside cathedral wall. These buttresses stood like ranks of soldiers putting their shoulders to the wall.

By 1163, buttresses had been around for centuries. Now a new twist was devised. The supporting walls, that is the buttresses, were constructed with large open spaces. The open space gave the buttress the appearance of a bridge, with a span across open air. A new name was given to them, flying buttress. They were called flying buttresses because their appearance gave them a sense of soaring, like birds flying high in the air. By supporting the outer walls with flying buttresses, openings could be cut within the walls to form large windows. These great windows were fitted with stained glass. Through their colored glass, light could flood in from above to represent the light of God. They also could be designed to tell biblical stories. Maurice knew all this because he too was a builder, not only of dreams, but of cathedrals as well.

The thoughts chilled Maurice with delight.

Meanwhile Brother Jacque had been watching Maurice. He was fascinated by Maurice's actions. After gazing at his fellow monk, Brother Jacque approached Maurice and his drawing.

"Whatever are you doing?" he asked.

"I am designing a great cathedral. The greatest in the land."

"Even greater than the cathedral in Chartres?" Jacque asked.

"Yes. Greater than any other."

Maurice returned to his earthen creation. He drew a large rectangle at the base of the cross. The outer dimensions extended past the north and south walls.

"This shall be the West Façade," he said with a nod. "The façade will serve as the front wall. It will contain three immense doors, many inches thick, that will welcome kings, courts, donors and common communicants alike. They will feel that they are entering into the presence of the Almighty. The cathedral must represent the Eternal City. Their thoughts must turn upward. Everything about the cathedral must point up to God. A great spire will crest over the roof that will point toward the heavens. Great windows fabricated of stained glass will adorn the walls from which light will flood in. The windows will tell of biblical stories that will teach the people. The people will sense they are entering into the divine presence of God."

His thoughts returned to the West Façade. He decided on two immense towers, standing as guardians. Each would be decorated elaborately as a gift to the Eternal Father. A wry smile broke across his face.

Then he spoke softly and resolutely to Brother Jacque. "Such towers will remind our parishioners of the power of the church. I fear the world of the twelfth century has become too secularized. It could cause the church to lose some of its power and influence. A few merchants are gaining wealth. Their money is new to them and they could use their wealth to obtain power, drawing some of the authority of the church away from the people. The church will have to join forces with the kings and powerful political forces in order to retain its power and authority. We have a powerful mission because ours is the one true church that must present itself to each villager as the greatest source of power in the world."

Maurice let the subject drop and returned to the drawing itself. He announced to Brother Jacque, "This cathedral shall be called Notre Dame, meaning Our Lady. It will be dedicated to the Mother of Our Lord. I think the name is most appropriate."

Maurice assembled builders and architects. Together they formulated plans that followed the new art movement known as the gothic style. This revolutionary design with pointed arches allowed the building to rise to dizzying heights.

Of course, Maurice knew his was a dream that he would never see completed. A cathedral of such magnitude would take many decades to complete. Generations of builders, each building on the shoulders of others, would be needed to finish the edifice.

Maurice began his work in 1163. It took nineteen years to complete the forward section of the cathedral. He was present when the altar was dedicated in May, 1182.

Work continued as builders constructed the rest of the nave, the flying buttresses, the spire and the great façade. All told, Notre Dame took more than a century to build.

It was the realization of a dream, first etched into the earth, by a man who would envision in his imagination what his eyes would never behold.

Author's note: While Maurice de Sully was a real person, Brother Jacque was fictitious.

III. Incident at Limoges, France

Guillaume de Limoges was moving quicker than his usual walking pace through the Poitou region of France. The cold, damp, dreary afternoon of the February day expressed his dismal spirit. He was determined that the grayness not dampen his pace. The man moved at a spirited tempo, hastened by the serious news he was about to deliver. The urgency of the news pushed him forward.

As he walked, he took notice of the changes of the land. He was seeing more farmland. "Why is that?" he asked himself. "Ah, yes, the forests are thinner. More and more our farmers are cutting down the trees. It will bring more food and prosperity to everyone."

Guillaume was a man who took note of new things. Laborers of the fields were using a newer and heavier plow developed by the people of China. Now the people of France would have more food. Wheat and beans would now be in abundance.

A Troubadour from the 13th Century

Guillaume turned his thoughts to the first hours when he would arrive in Poitiers. He would seek out the central market. It would be filled with people, eager to sell crops of the fields or goods made from wool. The place would be a mad mixture of people and animals. Dogs, chickens, pigs, goats, boys, girls, men, women; they'd all be there. He allowed himself to think of the luxuries of food he would eat. There would be peas and beans, nuts, berries, maybe even a bit of pork to add some bulk. The man was nearly famished. The food would do him good.

Following his feast, Guillaume would search for an open area, a place where scores of villagers could gather. Getting a following would not be a problem for him. He knew his fiddle, flute and bagpipe would draw attention. For years people had admired the surety of his performances. Villagers applauded his exceptional quality. His playing was always filled with emotion and a facility that dazzled. Surely, he thought, it would not take long for an excited crowd to gather. That made him smile. Singing and dancing would follow. Then he would tell his news.

The man of Limoges had unique talents and he was going to need them now. He was living life as a minstrel. Guillaume was a singing musician. His gifts did not stop there. He was a dancer and a bit of a jester too. He might even show off his abilities as a juggler. Mostly though, he was a wandering musical performer.

As he walked, Guillaume reviewed the melodious music Jean de Champagne had taught him months earlier. It was music that was tuneful, tinted by a touch of sadness. Guillaume had to admit that music so tuneful, yet sad, could be written only by one who was learned and skilled in the theories of music. Guillaume confessed to himself that Jean was a better writer of words and music that he. But that was because he was a literate man. Guillaume was not so lucky. Who was he? He was man hardly more than a serf. He owned no land. He bore no special honor. His birth gave him no special favors.

As a boy, Guillaume had developed an affinity for music. While the majority of the other boys learned the skills of the family, mostly producing goods made from wool, Guillaume taught himself to play the fiddle and flute. He also played the bagpipe, which he himself had made from the bladder of a sheep. With his strong, clear voice—pleasant, too, most would say—he could sing and make music. Now, as a man, his boyhood dreams of being the musician to the duke himself had come true.

Guillaume had enjoyed several years in service to the Duke of Limoges. As a minstrel, he performed his skills on the demands of the duke. In an instant, he could recall a large repertoire of tunes. He could perform happy music for weddings, feasts and dinners; while sad musings were left for quiet and intimate moments. He was ready with reflective melodies when the duke needed to be consoled or comforted. Provided that he performed his duties well, Guillaume was sure his services would to be retained.

After nearly five years of service to the duke, things changed. Jean de Champagne arrived in Limoges. His arrival had put Guillaume in a difficult position. Guillaume was a minstrel. On the other hand, Jean de Champagne was a troubadour. He was a new breed of poet-musician. Unfortunately for Guillaume, Jean enjoyed a higher status as a troubadour, a person who could write his own poetry and set it to his own music. One so learned as Jean was certain to create a problem for a minstrel like Guillaume.

Jean de Champagne arrived in Limoges scarred from the encounters and battles of the Third Crusade. He entered the village, not as a troubadour, but as a knight in armor. Like other knights, he had left his beloved France years earlier and journeyed to the Holy Lands on a great conquest. He joined the fight begun by the Pope who had challenged Christians to reclaim the Holy Lands. It was a struggle that had begun 300 years earlier when the Muslims conquered the lands Christ had walked 700 years before that.

Bad blood, envy and wars continued for centuries between the two religious forces. Each crusade pitted Muslim against Christian and Christian against Muslim. The Third Crusade had settled nothing. Jean feared more crusades would be necessary and the outcomes would not change much at all.

Jean's journey from the Holy Lands was a long and difficult one. His body was tired. Days of riding on horseback and long hours of simply walking beside his steed had wearied every bone in his body. Over and over in his mind, he replayed the events of the great battles. He could still recall the cries of women and children caught in the fighting. He had seen men disfigured. Towns and whole villages were ransacked, many burned to the ground. He had seen too much of it and now he was bringing the sad events back to Limoges. The news he had wasn't all that good. Still, he felt that it was his duty to report the truth of it.

Such thoughts dismayed him, yet he had reason to take personal comfort. He fought on the demand of the Pope. The Holy Father promised him, and the others who accepted the challenge, indulgences from past sins. Such indulgences meant he would receive mercy and leniency for the sins he had committed. It soothed some of the horrid memories.

The long trip gave him time to freshen his thoughts. Because Jean was a literate man with a knack for poetry, he fashioned his escapades into a poem. He organized the words by a natural-flowing rhythm. The lyrics followed with the regularity of a beating heart. The intensity of the words and rhythm suggested a rise and fall of tones which increased the passions of his thoughts. A tune began to develop in his ear.

When Jean set foot at Limoges, he was welcomed as a hero. Word spread quickly of his arrival. He told and sang of his warrior experiences. Whenever he sang, the news was intensified by the strength of his tunes. Jean understood the power of music to add dramatic emotion to his stories.

The Duke of Limoges was among the villagers who

were eager to hear word of the Third Crusade. The duke was impressed by two things. First, Jean's fine sense of duty as a knight. Second, his musical creations awed the nobleman. The duke also felt a responsibility to Jean because he had fought so valiantly for the church. He decided upon a suitable reward for the knight. He invited Jean to his luxurious home.

"Jean," the duke began, "you have brought honor to France and to the Holy Church. I wish to offer you a position worthy of your distinction."

"With all due grace, I thank you, my Lord," Jean responded while bowing.

"I have need of a poet and musician who will bring tuneful music and words of wisdom and comfort when I need them. I wish to offer you an appointment as court musician. You shall be considered a troubadour. That is the new word being bantered around. The word seems to have come from Spain to our south."

"While on the great crusade I was made aware of the Moors, the conquerors of Spain, who performed songs in such manner."

The duke replied, "Yes, I understand the Spanish borrowed the idea from these Middle Easterners."

Jean asked, "What are my duties to be, your Lord?"

"At my request, you shall write new lyrics, new songs and compose new music." Then adding with a delightful laugh, the duke continued. "I understand new expressions of courtly love to the ladies is quite acceptable these days. As you know, women of 1200 are receiving a higher respect than in the past. I concur with these developments that give honor to the ladies."

"Your Grace, I accept your kind offer. I promise to serve you well as a troubadour."

The duke dismissed Jean, who was delighted by the appointment.

However, the position stunned Guillaume. What would he do? He was but a mere minstrel, without training and uneducated. He was being replaced by Jean, a literate man with skills both as a poet and a musician. Guillaume asked for an audience with the duke. His request was granted. The meeting with the duke produced only thanks for his services, furthermore, he was told they were no longer needed. That left the lowly musician with no choice. Guillaume left Limoges and began wandering from village to village. All was not lost, he told himself, he was equipped with his instruments, a fine voice, talents as a juggler and his mind was abuzz with the latest news he had garnered in his travels.

Guillaume found himself walking his way into a new life as a minstrel. There were pleasant aspects to his new life. He enjoyed strolling the countryside, even with its constant dangers posed by robbers and thieves. Most of all, he took pleasure in meeting the people of each village. Upon his arrival in any town, he was greeted by townspeople eager to hear the news from other places. Since few, if any, of them could read, how else could they learn the rumors and information of distant lands? Guillaume found he had a purpose.

He turned his thoughts to his arrival at Poitiers. He expected to be greeted by villagers, then he would deliver some of his news. Certainly, they would offer him a hearty meal in exchange for some good gossip. He was sure he could depend on the butcher and baker for some fine free food. After delivering his news, he would pull out his musical instruments and break into a lively gigue. Then an evening of festivities would follow. The raucous tone of his bagpipe was certain to precipitate a crowd of interested folks. Then he would pull out his fiddle to provide an excellent accompaniment to village dances. Later in the evening when the fires calmed to embers, he would play his flute. Its clear tones would bring a hush to the night air. The minstrel knew he had all the equipment and skills required to keep each villager captivated.

These thoughts lifted his spirits and carried him onward. Guillaume paused for a drink at an open brook. The raw winter's day cut to the bone. He was chilled. Though he wasn't particular thirsty, he understood the need to take in as much water as possible. He still had a good distance to cover before nightfall.

As he dipped his cupped hands into the frigid waters, he heard voices. They were raised and animated. Guillaume guessed they were about two-hundred paces away. Fearing beggars, or worse, robbers, he quickly took refuge behind a large boulder. Waiting in absolute silence, the minstrel waited for sight of the travelers.

His tense muscles relaxed when Guillaume took note that both wanderers were carrying instruments. They resembled his. He darted from behind the rock, greeted his new friends and immediately the trio embarked on a wild conversation. News and questions passed back and forth.

"Have you heard the latest on the Crusades?"

"What news can you tell of the new cathedral in Paris?"

"Will it be named 'Notre Dame' for the Mother of Our Lord?"

"Is it true Richard the Lionhearted has been captured? Surely not!"

Guillaume's luck had turned to good fortune. News he gathered from his new friends would bring him respect in any village. Of course, they pumped him for his news, which he offered. Guillaume was careful not to give away too much spicy information. That he would keep to himself. After half an hour, the trio parted ways, though Guillaume would have preferred to tarry and catch up on all the latest hearsay. His mission, though, nagged on his mind. He knew his time was limited with his fellow minstrels. Bidding adieu, he took his leave and stepped up his pace.

Darkness falls early in February. The air grows more chilled as the afternoon wanes. The dampness urged him on. Guillaume first caught sight of Poitiers as the sullen skies grew first gray, then charcoal and finally black.

"At last!" he exclaimed out loud, though no one was around to hear. The thought that he was talking to himself didn't bother him. He decided if no one heard him, what matter did it make? On the other hand, if he had been heard and thought to be silly, what matter was that to him? Catching a glimpse of the city had lifted his spirits.

He hurried toward the city, increasing his pace. Then he hesitated. He thought, "If I arrive after dark, who will greet me?" His mind kept spinning. "Of what importance will I be if no on sees me enter. I would be far better off if I arrived at mid-morning. Then the village will be alive with activity."

Guillaume took refuge in a small grove of trees. He put his back against a rock, closed his eyes as the evening light escaped. He dreamed of the things he would tell the people of Poitiers. Richard the Lionhearted had been captured. Worse yet, rumor was that he would be executed. Such news would be a shock to everyone. He would also tell them of a remarkable story about a place called China. The people of China had built a pagoda that stood sixty meters high. It was one-hundred, ninety-six feet from floor to roof. Not only that, but it was still standing thirty-five years later. He would save the best for last. Had they heard that Pope Innocent II declared the marriage of Frances's King Phillip II to Agnes of Merania to be null and void? He would tell them that the Pontiff declared Phillip was still married to Ingeborg, daughter of King Valdemar of Denmark. "What a scandal!" he thought. The people would ask him if Phillip would leave Agnes. What would he tell them?

He could hardly wait for the night to pass.

Author's Note: Guillaume de Limoges, Jean de Champagne and the Duke of Limoges were fictitious persons.

IV. Incident at Venice

Ottaviano Petrucci warmed his hands by the fire. Working with the metal of his printing press had left his fingers numb from the Venetian chill. The man complained that this winter had been one of the coldest he'd seen. On his way to market the day before, he had observed ice on the shores of the Lagoon of Venice. That proved how bitter it was. Though the cold chilled him, it didn't slow his determination.

"The fire feels good, doesn't it?" commented Pietro, the young assistant Petrucci had tutored for the past two years

Yes," he told Pietro, "but I can't dally by the fire too long. My work keeps calling me."

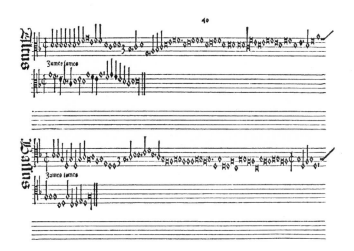

Odhecaton, 1501

Petrucci, like a good businessman, was driven by the urgency of the work itself. He had often wondered who worked who? Did the work work him? Or did he work for the work itself? Even he was confused by such thinking.

Whatever it was, he had been toiling on his project for nearly three years now. The immensity of printing a hundred chansons had not seemed so huge when he began. However, he found himself having to practically invent a variety of innovations. Printing *music* was more than printing *words*. It began with the printing of lines of the staff, then the text. Finally, the notes had to be processed. All had to be done in succession and independently. These steps were only a part of the many problems. Petrucci had to decide with great care which compositions were worthy of print. He hadn't even given much thought to how he would bring the books to the open market.

"That will wait for the right time," he told himself. "Being the first isn't easy," he had often reminded Pietro.

The fire felt so good he thought a few extra minutes by its warmth wouldn't matter too much. The flames mesmerized him. A blank stare fell across his face. His mind became engaged in thoughts that carried him back to the start of his heroic task. The reminiscences took him back to the beginning, a career that began eleven years earlier in 1490. Taking his eyes off the fire, he looked at Pietro who was carefully setting the movable metal types in place. He could see the apprentice was doing good work.

"The work, do you like it?" questioned Petrucci.

"Very much. It is slow and painstaking, but I think it shall do much good for the people," Pietro responded.

Petrucci was impressed by the depth of Pietro's comment. Yes, a printer like he, could agree composers and musicians would profit greatly when his book was completed. Because they were in the trade, they would benefit the most. Pietro's comment offered something new. His remark suggested that every literate person could gain an advantage by obtaining a book of printed music. He found that the boy's perceptions were quite remarkable.

Petrucci grew excited. "Pietro, you will not believe what our project will do for music. Books with words alone have been printed on the press for nearly half a century. As a result, great learning has already taken place because of these books, much of it outside the Holy Church. Certainly, you've seen how greatly the world has been changed by the press. Why should music be left behind?" With a glowing look, he proceeded. "I sense our printing project will change music. It will open new worlds to composers. I believe this with certainty."

"Master," Pietro said with a deep sense of reverence, "I, too, believe in your vision. To be part of it gives me happiness."

Laughing, Petrucci told him, "Some day you will set up your own shop. Don't do it here in Venice. I don't need the competition." Petrucci didn't mean that in a harmful way. He merely had gained a healthy respect for his young assistant and could see a wonderful future for the lad.

"Senor Petrucci, tell me how this project came about."

Petrucci could sense the spirit of the entrepreneur in the request. He could also smell competition in the future. Still, he decided the boy could benefit from his experience. He began his story.

"I was born in Fossombrone."

"Isn't that about a 100 kilometers south of Venice?" asked Pietro. "I've heard winters are warmer there."

Nodding that it was, Petrucci continued. "I was educated in Urbino. I was ambitious, a young man ready to take on all of Italy. When I was a bit older than you, twenty-four or so,

I moved to Venice to learn the art of printing." Petrucci pressed on. "Two developments struck me like a bolt of lightning: paper and the press. I could see that since the process of making paper had been discovered and that Herr Gutenberg had developed a printing press with movable type, there was a good profit to be made in the printing industry. A great many people of Europe began demanding books which they saw as essential tools for learning. They insisted on secular books as well as sacred ones."

"For the church and the universities both, right?" asked Pietro.

"Exactly."

The young boy amazed Petrucci.

"Let me tell you how great the need was. In 1424, that is hardly more than seventy years ago, Cambridge University had only 122 books. Think of that! Just 122 books for a great center of learning. I ask you. How sad is that?" Now his voice began rising, reaching a higher pitch with every word. "Catch this. Each book in that library had the value of a farm or a vineyard."

Pietro's jaw dropped.

Petrucci could see the eagerness in his young friend. He continued with boisterous zeal. "Gutenberg did great work as he and others invented the printing press. There is no question to that. However, a printing press would be like a carriage without a horse."

"What do you mean?" asked Pietro.

"Paper! That's what I mean?"

"Paper? I don't get it."

"Paper changed everything. Paper replaced parchment."

"Of course, I know that," said Pietro, shaking his head at his own disappointment. He had wanted to impress his master with his knowledge. He was upset by missing the opportunity.

Petrucci began his explanation. "Parchment had been used for centuries, but it is so expensive to produce. There is a great deal that goes into making parchment. Skin of calves, sheep or goats have to be extracted, processed, then dried. That's not all. It is difficult to work with. It wrinkles. Humidity affects it." He threw up his hands in mock frustration. "Gutenberg and the others," raising his finger, "they created type that was movable. They used metal, not wood for the type. Metal is more permanent than wood. But more importantly, metal type produced a text that was clear to the eye." Shoving his hands together until they were clasped, he said, "When paper and the printing press came together, books could be produced cheaply. Demand for books exploded! Ah, what great work Gutenberg had done!"

Pietro became as excited as his master. "I, too, want to be part of it!"

"Yes, my boy, I think you shall. Now let's get back to work and complete chanson number 91 before this day is through."

"That will make it nine more songs to go," Pietro said with a smile.

Hours later, well after the setting of the sun while the light of the candles was growing tiresome to their weary eyes, Petrucci turned to his apprentice. "Pietro, run to the market, and buy us some fish and vegetables for roasting."

Minutes later the boy returned with the food. It was cooked over the fire and a lively conversation ensued.

Pietro was ready for more. "Tell me, Master, what was it like to petition the Prince of Venice? I understand he can be difficult."

Pietro's question brought back the memories. With a heavy sigh, Petrucci began the story of his great project to create a volume of printed music. Before he could even consider setting up his shop to print music, he needed to receive permission from the prince. It was not an easy request.

"I applied to the Doge, as he is known, for the exclusive right to print music."

Pietro stopped him. "What do you mean by 'exclusive'?"

"Exclusive means that no one else could be allowed to print music. It would be a right granted to me alone, without competition. It was a great favor I was asking. But I was earnest." He added in a whisper. "I could see the money that was to be made. I was not about to be turned down."

Pietro had already learned that Petrucci had been granted his right two years before the two had joined forces. Still he had other questions.

"When did you begin your apprenticeship as a printer?"

Petrucci told him, "I was an apprentice for eight years." He said it again. "Eight years I spent learning the art of the press."

"Tell me more about the Doge himself," Pietro urged.

Petrucci pondered, then continued. "Although he seemed impressed by the idea of printing music, I was unsure if he would agree. I reminded him that I knew of no music that had been printed on the press. He said that if a man in the profession did not know of printed music, how could he know of such manuscript? Right there, right then, he granted me the exclusive right to print music."

"Was that *it*?" asked Pietro.

"Oh, no. The right was good for twenty years. No more."

"How did you begin?"

"Oh, there were obstacles. I had to carve notes into the tin or other metal blocks. Notes of all kinds. Some in the shape of diamonds. Some with stems. Some white notes for the long-held values. Some blackened for shorter rhythms." He raised his voice to indicate the frustrations. "Then there were the dots. There were clefs to create. Symbols for the *musica ficta* had to be fashioned. I had to create a separate plate for the lines of the staff. Yet another plate for the text." He bonked himself on the forehead with his open palm for dramatic effect.

"You must have been overwhelmed, or at least discouraged at times," Pietro said with understanding.

"It was like inventing the wheel again and again," Petrucci told him. "You have little idea!"

The remark smarted Pietro. Petrucci saw the injury he had done to the boy. The realization calmed him down. "No, my son, I think you would understand the frustrations."

"For me," Pietro said, "it is the three separate tasks that I find so difficult."

Petrucci contemplated the trials he had faced. "Yes, I discovered that the lines that would hold the notes had to be printed first. I found that the oil-based ink that Gutenberg had used worked quite well, even for each musical staff. With the musical lines on the paper, I could print the words. Finally, I could print the music last of all. Imagine that. The notes came last. Adding the music was the final step. Thank goodness I did not have to align the text with the notes. Good musicians are trained to do that on their own." Petrucci reminded the boy a last time. "Three times we must send them through the press." He kicked the leg of his press to make his point.

Pietro added, "Getting all three printings lined up, that is what takes the time. That doesn't start to express the difficulty."

"Expensive too," added Petrucci. He shrugged his shoulders. "Being the first…"

Petrucci started the sentence, while his assistant finished it, "isn't easy."

Petrucci laughed.

"Well," Pietro wondered, "I may understand the process of printing, but what about the music? How did you choose the composers, the pieces, the music that would be printed? These would have to be significant works, would they not?"

Petrucci was astounded by the boy's intuitions.

"Pietro, I understood history was in the making. The choices were most difficult. I began with works composed about thirty years ago. They were somewhat old fashioned because they were composed for three voices. Then I found more complex and up-to-date works of four voices to complete the volume. I selected music of the Burgundian composers. That is because musicians of the Lowlands and the north of France are excellent writers of music. They deserved to be included."

"What will become of the book?" asked Pietro.

"I believe a volume of chansons will provide music for many composers to enjoy and to study. I see new developments happening in music. The crisp, harmonious music of our Italian composers, which, as you know, is simple in its texture will become the source for all music. Composers will learn how to combine the delights of Italian music with the more complex music of composers from the north. A great flowering of music will take place."

Pietro took it in with pride. He was a part of it all.

Several months later the book was completed. Together, Petrucci and Pietro reviewed the first copy with great relish. Petrucci spent most of the first hour clutching the copy next to his chest. Finally he put the book down, which was immediately snatched up by Pietro. The apprentice spent the rest of the day checking the binding, reviewing each composition, checking the clarity of the thousands of notes. He, as a student, was as proud of the volume as his teacher. Both glowed with satisfaction. Each work was accurate. Before retiring for the day, Pietro decided the tome deserved one more look. Admiringly, he remarked to Petrucci, "Good clean work." He put the book down and admired its title, *Harmonice Musices Odhecaton*. He was impressed and said so. "Amazing! It is the first book of printed music."

"Really, it is the first book of polyphonic music. That means it is music of many lines, not merely a collection of melodies or teaching tunes," corrected Petrucci.

The boy couldn't help himself. One more look, he decided. Flicking through the pages front to back, a sudden look of horror grew over his face. "No," he said to himself, "this can't be right!"

He scanned the pages again. This time his efforts were slow and methodical. They confirmed his fears. Quickly moving to Petrucci, Pietro exclaimed, "Master, we are in error!"

"What?!" burst out Petrucci.

"There are only 96 songs in our book, *Harmonice Musices Odhecaton*. The musicians will expect 100 chansons. The word *odhecaton* means 100!"

Pausing for only a moment, the master printer pronounced, "Then we simply shall not tell them."

The remark brought a wry smile to his face.

Author's note: While Ottaviano Pettruci was a real person, Pietro, his assistant, was fictitious.

V. Incident at St. Mark's Cathedral in Venice

The year was 1609. The German composer Heinrich Schutz was approaching Venice, the famed city of canals. Though his spirits were aglow with excitement, his stomach was as rigid as a seaman's sheepshank knot. He suppressed the tightness in his gut and asked directions to St. Mark's Square.

He approached a man guiding a long narrow boat. "St. Mark's Cathedral? Where can I find it?" Schutz had been practicing his northern Italian dialect and here was his chance to try it out.

Gilberto, a gondolier, was familiar with the various accents of many travelers. Venice was a city used to the continual entourage of tourists from every direction, particularly of German, Dutch, English and French descent.

St. Mark's Cathedral

Gilberto hollered back, "Right in the middle of the city. Can't miss it!" Not missing a business opportunity, "For a small price, I'll take you there. Hand me a tip and I'll give you a guided tour."

Though short on cash from his long journey from his homeland, Schutz replied, "I would appreciate the introduction to your famed city."

Heinrich hopped on the gondola and rode the canals of Italy's most unusual city. Gilberto was more than a gondolier. He was an entertainer too. Between the singing of airs from a recently-composed opera called *Orfeo*, Gilberto pointed out the unique sights of Venice.

"Venice is actually a city that stretches across more than 100 islands. It has a long history too. Why the city was the staging ground for the Crusades! It is known the world around as the 'City of Water.' It was also home to the greatest navy in the world."

Schutz asked his burning question. "What keeps the buildings from crumbling into the Aegean Sea? How can they be built on water?"

Gilberto had heard the question asked a thousand times from a thousand visitors.

"Venice isn't built on the sea, nor are the buildings floating. The city is built on a series of more than 100 islands. The land of the islands supports the buildings. Canals flow between the islands. These rivers of the sea became perfectly suited as streets. They offer an easy way to transport goods and people. Best of all, no horses to smell up the place."

Heinrich Schutz wasn't too impressed by the horrific odors coming from the canals.

"Stinks just like every other city I've traveled through."

Heinrich's comment was true. The canals were a disgusting soup of trash, debris and the waste of animals and humans.

"Throw it in the canal and let the sea carry it away," Gilberto told him.

Heinrich was eager to learn more about St. Mark's. "What about the cathedral itself? What can you tell me?"

"Oh my! St. Mark's has quite a history. It was begun in 828. Then a new church was built four years later. In 976, the church was burned in a rebellion, then rebuilt two years later. The cathedral was finally completed nearly a century after that and consecrated in 1094."

All this fascinated Schutz.

Gilberto said, "It is unlike other European churches because Venice is a mixture of Eastern and Western cultures. Turks, Greeks, Arabs have come here. They brought their architectural ideas. The men who designed and built St. Mark's used those cultures in the design. It is unique in all of Europe, don't you think?"

Heinrich's first view of St. Mark's overwhelmed him. "Amazing. Simply amazing," he kept uttering.

Approaching St. Mark's Square, Schutz could hear the loud cackling of doves. Gilberto announced, "All those pigeons make quite a racket. Everyday they will welcome you to the cathedral. But watch where you step. Avoid all the white slippery spots." He waved a hearty goodbye to his new friend.

Schutz came to Venice in order to meet one of the most famed organists and composers of the day. The 24-year old German composer was also about to meet the most original-thinking composer of all Europe. He had come to study composition with Giovanni Gabrieli, one of the most respected of all composers in Europe. He held the appointment as Chapelmaster of the magnificent St. Mark's Cathedral in Venice. It was a coveted honor.

Schutz stood on the great square admiring the magnificent structure. The exterior was a mix of rounded domes. The roof was decorated with an array of spires. A series of arched doorways welcomed parishioners and visitors. Above it all, St. Mark's exuded the flavor of the Orient.

After pausing to admire its exterior, Schutz moved toward the great edifice. In quiet reverence, he entered the Cathedral of Venice. He could hear voices. They echoed and resounded over and again in the marbled chambers. He looked up and saw one of the two choir lofts the church was famous for. A second loft was placed at the opposite of the other. Schutz reminded himself that Adrian Willaert, the esteemed Dutch composer, had begun a new style of polychoral singing right here at St. Mark's. He created music that contrasted two separate choirs, each placed in one of the lofts.

"So this the place of antiphonal choirs," he whispered to a priest who had just arisen from his prayers.

The priest replied, "Antiphonal singing is a tradition from the Eastern Orthodox Church. Capellmeister Gabrieli uses it to great advantage. You know he is the finest choral master in the world." Adding in a quieter tone, "Finer, I think, than his uncle Andreas, who himself was an exceptional choirmaster."

Heinrich gave an understanding nod.

Schutz had come prepared to stay in Venice for a period of three years. Diligently, he spent his time copying and studying the compositions of Gabrieli. He used the time to improve his already significant organ talents with lessons with the Venetian master.

Although Schutz was nervous at first, a healthy respect developed between the two. Gabrieli opened up to Schutz.

"I'm fortunate to be here," Giovanni had remarked to his fellow composer. He admitted that he had won his position by the luck of his birth. Giovanni's uncle had served as Chapelmaster until his death. After his uncle's demise, Giovanni won the audition over the hopes of many worthy composers. The position offered good pay and high recognition. It brought him great esteem.

"Chapelmaster, tell me about your most famous work, the *Sonata Pian' e Forte,*" Schutz asked of Gabrieli. He had been eager to ask the question. Having proved himself a worthy composer, Heinrich felt he could pose the question.

"It was in 1597," Giovanni began. "I was composing my *Sacre Symphonie*, a church work for instruments. I wanted to create a work that emphasized the great contrasts of music. The 6 ½ second reverberation of the cathedral was giving me a problem. Whenever I composed music in the Roman tradition, which as you know is complex and thick, the sound was overwhelming. Such an echo! The complex music kept getting jumbled. In the Roman tradition, many lines are combined simultaneously. The overlapping lines cause confusion. The music lacks clarity. It is like a madhouse of too many people having too many conversations all at the same time. I thought it would be more effective to create blocks of sound that were unified by a pleasant and sonorous quality. Then an idea came to me. I could contrast choirs of instruments in the same fashion as choirs of voices. These could echo each other in the antiphonal setting that the great master Adrian Willaert had began decades earlier. The effect was dramatic and immediate." Proudly he added, "I believe it will be a device that other composers will use."

Schutz knew for certain that he would employ this device of contrasting dynamics when he returned to his homeland. He had another question for the master.

"Wasn't it in this piece, the *Sonata Pian' e Forte,* that you first specified which instrument was to play each part?"

"Quite novel of an idea, don't you think?"

"More than novel, it was revolutionary."

"In the score, I indicated that two instrumental choirs were to be created. One choir was to include one cornett and three sackbuts. The second choir consisted of a violin and three sackbuts. I was certain that the timbre of the cornett and that of the violin would be sufficiently different to contrast one from the other."

Schutz requested, "Tell me of the dynamics."

"I wanted to heighten the contrast between the choirs. I specifically marked in the score the volume of sound the ensemble was to play. For quiet passages I wrote *piano*. That is our Italian term for soft. For the loud passages I marked *forte*. *Forte* is our Italian word for loud."

Continuing with his story, Giovanni said, "Since the Council of Trent in 1563, the music of the church has taken a significantly different course than music of the secular world. Sacred music is hushed and deeply rooted in the intellect. It is constructed only of limited emotions. It is quiet and reverent. That is rightfully so in worship to God. However, I believe it is also beyond the comprehension of most people. That's not all. For nearly each service, the music is freshly composed. Composers are expected to create new music. That causes a problem for the congregants. Rarely is there a common man who can understand it. The music proscribed by the Council might be reverent, even beautiful, it is also too complex for the masses. I wanted to create music that was simpler, easier to grasp. I also intended to create a music far more powerful too. Power and emotions are the forces preferred by the Venetian people."

Schutz began to see that Giovanni Gabrieli was not only a great composer, he was an original thinker as well. He could see that the master was a mover and shaker. If other composers were to employ Gabrieli's innovations, music was certain to change.

Gabrieli continued with his discussion. "I wanted the listener to become bathed in the music. I decided to place one choir of musical instruments in one loft and contrast that choir with voices and instruments. With the great reverberation in St. Mark's, it was necessary to create a simpler kind of music. The Venetians are in love with music that impresses, overpowers and is colorful. It is a reflection of our unique culture blending the East and West. All these thoughts I brought together in the *Sonata Pian' e Forte.*"

Then he added in a whisper, "You know how conservative they are in Rome. Backwards, I would say! Hardly anything new comes out of the Roman Church. Venice is the city of innovation."

Schutz spent three productive years in Venice then returned to his German homeland. The remainder of his days were spent creating a new kind of music that combined the ideals of the Venetian master with Schutz's beloved German traditions. His music became a model for Johann Sebastian Bach decades later.

Author's note: Only Gilberto, the gondolier, was a fictitious person.

VI. Incident at Lubeck, Germany

Dieterich's first view of the city of Lubeck was one he knew he would never forget. The great series of spires across the city had a dramatic impact on him. A sweep of his eyes showed him a significant number of slender fingers pointing directly upward. Rising to heights above them all were the twin spires of St. Mary's Church. As a symbol of both ecclesiastical and political power, St. Mary's two vertical giants each towered more than 400 feet above the streets of Lubeck. Their lean appearance thrust the eye of the beholder toward the heavens above. They also hinted at the wealth of its merchants below

The spires stood as guardians over the port city of Lubeck on the Baltic Sea. They offered hope to a city constantly bathed in overcast, dreary and freezing weather. The people of Lubeck suffered through long and dark winters, given added chill by frosty sea breezes. Villagers took comfort in the hope the church gave them. St. Mary's twin guardians were visible signs that offered warmth to the soul when the body could feel only the chill.

Dieterich Buxtehude

The roots of St. Mary's Church date back to the 13th century. By 1200, Lubeck had become a city of significant importance and power with wealthy merchants trading goods throughout the known world. The Town Council of 1226 wanted a structure that was a symbol of free will to remote buyers and displayed the world power of the city. Over the next generation, plans were made to construct a church built to nearly insurmountable proportions. In 1250, work was begun on the edifice that would include two towers, hundreds of feet tall, standing over a main chapel with a vaulted ceiling reaching 125 feet over the floor. A stacking of twelve stories would not have touched its ceiling. It was the to be tallest brick vault in Europe. Its significance was not to be overlooked.

Lubeck was a northern German city that enjoyed the status of being the Queen City of the Hanseatic League. Because it was the center of trade of nearly all the North Sea, a number of merchants gained their wealth by trading wax, resin, timber and furs. Inside its city limits were a number of churches. St. Mary's Church was the largest and most important.

St. Mary's was an important musical center. However the church suffered a great loss in December, 1667. Choirmaster Franz Lunder died and a suitable replacement was needed. The Church Council was in agreement that due to the importance of the church in such a distinguished city as Lubeck, only the finest organist and choirmaster would do. The candidate would also be expected to compose organ works that would bring considerable regard to the newly renovated organ.

Thomas Notke, president of the Church Council, began the meeting. "Gentlemen, I anticipate we shall have no problem finding applicants for the position of Organmaster, yet we must secure the services of only the finest."

"And the pay," requested the treasurer Herrmann Gratz, "shall it be considerable?"

On that, there was no doubt. All agreed that the Choirmaster's salary should be high enough to entice the finest organist available. The call for a new Choirmaster went forth.

Notice of the esteemed position attracted the attention of an organist by the name of Dieterich Buxtehude who was born in Denmark. At the time, he was serving as organist at a church in the city of Elsinore. He was an excellent organist and made a positive impression at his audition for the St. Mary's position.

As Council president, Notke favorably commented, "Herr Buxtehude, the committee is stirred by your performances. You demonstrate great command of your fingers on the manuals of the organ. You also seem to have a new awareness of the importance of the pedals. We encourage you to develop compositions along these lines."

A special request was made of the new Organmaster, conveyed by Notke. "We will expect you to carry on the tradition of *Abendmusik* begun under the former Organmaster."

Buxtehude was familiar with the musical services performed in the month prior to the Christmas season. It was begun by the former organist, Franz Tunder. Word had spread throughout the protestant churches about these performances. They attracted attention to the church.

Buxtehude told the committee, "I heartily agree. Each of the five Sundays before Christmas, a concert of music worthy of God will echo within the walls of St. Mary's. I will compose new music for the organ, instruments and the choir. It will be an honor to do so."

"One more matter," Johann Bernham asked, "are you willing to accept the allegiance to our land? It will be necessary to take the oath, given that you are from outside our city." Buxtehude agreed and took the oath.

Buxtehude gladly accepted the offer at a pay that was nearly equal to the Pastor's salary, a remarkable indication of the favorable impression he'd made on the Council. When he accepted the post as Choirmaster of St. Mary's, it was his third appointment. The first two positions had established his reputation as both a fine organist and a promising composer who followed the traditions of Lutheran composers. His audition had thoroughly impressed the whole Council. His lifelong relationship with St. Mary's was cemented when he married Tunder's daughter. Seven daughters, of which three survived to adulthood, came from their union.

Buxtehude performed his duties admirably. He was the perfect complement to a city proclaimed as the Queen of the Hanseatic League. Lubeck was the central city of all of the states and port cities throughout the North Sea region. It also housed the largest church, St. Mary's. The combination of the great composer Buxtehude, the importance of St. Mary's Church and the commercially powerful city of Lubeck became the magnets that attracted attention throughout Germany. Such a distinguished combination inspired Buxtehude to set the highest standards for himself. As a result, his reputation grew. Young composers, organists and musicians eager to hear the finest music would travel great distances to be in his presence. They were likely to attend the services of the *Abendmusik*.

Buxtehude's tenure at St. Mary's continued for decades.

On this particular winter's evening in 1697, as the 17th century was closing, Buxtehude, who had now passed his sixtieth birthday, was in the midst of his preparations for Advent Services. Tonight was the third concert of *Abendmusik* at St. Mary's. It was in the middle of the five-concert series and Christmas was quickly approaching. After Sunday morning services, the Organmaster had returned home for dinner. He had hoped for a restful afternoon before the evening service. Dinner was hardly the respite he had hoped it would be.

Anna, his oldest daughter, was whining about the meal her mother had prepared. With a voice that had the edge of a woodsmen's axe, she told her mother, "Must we have pork again? Every Sunday it's the same. I'm sick of it."

"Now, Anna, you don't have to eat it if you don't like it. How many times have I told you that you only have to eat what you like?"

Anna demanded in a voice that raised the temperature of the room several degrees, "Mother, why is it I'm always stuck here on every Sunday having dinner with you and father? I have no life of my own. Every week, it's Sunday service, Sunday dinner—and it's ALWAYS pork—then help father with HIS work! Why can't I have a life of my own?"

The words were the same week after week.

Frau Buxtehude had developed the habit of spoiling Anna. The loss of their other daughters had grieved her so much she endured her sorrows by giving in to Anna's many whims. She required little housework from Anna, let her sleep to all hours of the morning, and even made her bed for her after she arose. Anna was lazy, whiney and expected the world to adapt to her caprices.

After a short nap, Buxtehude decided to walk to St. Mary's Church for the *Abendmusik* service. Anna joined him.

"Let's walk past the docks," Anna demanded.

"All right. The fresh air will feel good." Buxtehude agreed though his heart wasn't in it. His mind was on the upcoming service.

The sea air was raw after covering hundreds of miles across the cold Baltic Sea. It cut sharply into their faces. The air was also filled with the stench of the fish markets on the docks. They hurried, seeking some relief from both the chill and the odors. They moved past the market and on to the magnificence of the town hall on the their way to St. Mary's.

The dinner had left Anna with a nauseating sensation

in her stomach. It put her in a foul mood. As they walked, a cat crossed their path. She kicked it.

"Why did you kick the poor creature?" Buxtehude asked.

"Why not? It got in my way."

Remarks and actions like these were commonplace with Anna. They drove Buxtehude to do much thinking. "Who would accept her as a wife?" The thought was hardly far from his mind.

As they walked, a plan formulated in his head. To make it work, he would probably need the approval of the church council. He was sure they would agree. He had done favors for them in the past.

He thought, "I have played for their weddings. Wasn't I there for the baptism of their children? Did I not provide music in their moments of grief when they lost their own children? Who was it but I who taught their children clavichord lessons and the theories of music? I am sure if I solicit their favor, they will grant it." He decided to give his scheme time to develop.

Anna broke his train of thought. She pleaded, "Hurry up! The wind is so rough and I'm freezing."

Dieterich asked, "Did you arrange for the calcant to meet us at the church?"

"Yes, of course. What do you take me for? A fool? The calcant promised to be at St. Mary's two hours before the service. If he's not on time, I'll let him have it."

Anna was an excellent detail person. And a no nonsense person as well. He knew that if the calcant wasn't on time, or didn't perform his duties adequately, he was certain to meet up with Anna's wrath. The calcant knew it too because he had been the recipient of her anger in the past. It was quite unpleasant.

Buxtehude told her, "You know how much I need the services of the calcant to pump the bellows of the organ. The organ will not operate without him. His job is to fill the bellows that activate the air that supplies the airflow to the organ pipes. The organ is useless without the calcant. I have done all the preparatory finger work on the clavichord, so I need the organ in order to rehearse the music I've written for the pedals."

Anna cut him off. "Father, I know all this. Do you take me for a child?"

"Anna, I have been in the position as Chapelmaster for more than thirty years, but I cannot rest on the past. There are fine composers and organists from the south who travel here to Lubeck to hear the music I compose. Nothing can be left to chance."

Once inside, Buxtehude moved directly to the great pipe organ. It was a fine instrument though it was not excessively large. It consisted of two manuals and a full pedal board. It's most recent renovation by Friedrich Stellwagen half a century earlier, had proven to be an inspiration to the composer.

As an organist, Buxtehude's performances were renowned for great facility and technique of the hands. His manual playing was clear and precise. It didn't stop there. He had also developed considerable foot facility. This gave him ample opportunity to create a pedal line nearly as significant and important as the music for the hands. It was considerably more developed than the Italians who neither had the desire nor interest in developing such foot technique. Simplicity and clarity were their goals. Why bother to cloud the spirit of music? German composers, embracing the spirit of the Reformation, aimed at a more serious music reflective of their worship needs. Buxtehude followed the German tradition.

Two young gentlemen were seen entering the sanctuary well ahead of the service. Anna guessed their ages at about eighteen or so. One of the gentlemen (she believed his friend called him George) was particularly handsome and tall. She thought he carried himself in a pompous sort of way.

"Probably his tallness that gives him that superiority complex," she thought.

Following the service, the two gentlemen moved to the organ, hoping to meet Buxtehude, who was quite used to receiving acclaim and attention. He liked it. He agreed to meet them for a few moments.

George was the first to speak. "Herr Buxtehude, we are honored to hear you this evening. Even in the blasted cold of the December night, I am impressed with the flexibility of your fingers. They move with such dexterity and clarity."

Johann, the other young man, offered comments directed more towards the structure of the music. "I was most impressed by your compositions. There is a balance and freedom of form within each piece. Your organ works display great richness of character and musical understanding. It has been an honor to hear you perform and to meet you as well."

Buxtehude thanked the two gentlemen for their kind words. He inquired, "Do you plan to remain in Lubeck for long?"

"For some weeks, I should think," George told him.

"Do come see me during the days when services are not being held and I shall be happy to answer any questions you have. I assume you are musicians? Perhaps we might have dinner together."

The shorter caller introduced himself. "Herr Chapelmaster, I am Johann Matteson."

His friend followed suit. "I am George Frederick Handel."

Buxtehude suggested they all meet later for a lively discussion about music. Buxtehude was particularly intrigued by George, a handsome man of considerable talent he was certain. Buxtehude's developing idea once again surfaced to his consciousness.

Within a week Buxtehude could not help himself. He called George Handel aside. "Are you interested in this position I hold? A strong recommendation from me could guarantee you the position."

Handel was intrigued.

"There is one matter I must tell you," Buxtehude said.

"What is it?"

"The position will go to the man who agrees to marry my daughter Anna."

The proposition hit Handel like the rock that impacted the forehead of Goliath. He'd seen and heard enough of her.

"She's as pleasant as a mule," Handel thought to himself.

Anna gave George a reason for him to make a pledge that he would remain a single man for life. It was one promise he kept to his dying day.

Both men left Lubeck the next day. No position was worth that!

Two years later another young man named Johann, about twenty years of age, left the city of Arnstadt for a journey to Lubeck he estimated would take about a month. With little or no money, it would have to be done on foot and it would cover two-hundred, fifty miles. He journeyed to hear the famed Buxtehude. When he arrived, he thrilled to the music he heard. Days went by, weeks passed, the man was a bundle of questions which he peppered to Buxtehude. Johann bought every score of Buxtehude's organ music he could locate. He studied the music with the focus of a lion on its prey.

Johann lingered on at Lubeck hoping to grasp the greatness of Buxtehude's music. Finally, with fear that he might lose his own position, Johann prepared to depart for Arnstadt. He checked his boots. They were in for thousands and thousands of steps.

Before leaving, Buxtehude called Johann to his studio. "Young Johann, I have a proposal for you. You are an exceptionally fine organist. I believe you are the finest organist in all of Germany. I am an old and feeble man and will leave this post soon. I have the power to see that you could hold my post."

Johann was intrigued and interested in hearing more.

"There is one matter. Should you accept the post, you will be required to marry Anna, my oldest daughter. Are you interested?"

Johann met her one time. That was enough. "Ah....Ah...No, Herr Buxtehude, I am not interested in your post. I merely came to hear you play."

He was on him way back to Arnstadt the next morning.

Upon his arrival at his home, the Church Council immediately called Johann in for a serious reprimand. "You were given a one-month leave. You took three. Why have you acted in such a cavalier manner?"

"I only tarried to study and hear the music of the greatest composer I know. His name is Dieterich Buxtehude. I felt I could learn much from him."

"That may be true, but we almost gave away your position. Your enormous talent saved you. We will continue to honor your appointment but, don't ever let it happen again!"

Johann promised. "It won't."

"If you do, you will lose this position! Is that clear, Mr. Johann Sebastian Bach?"

"Perfectly clear," he said.

Author's note: Only the members of the Church Council were fictitious, including Thomas Notke, Herrmann Gratz and Johann Bernham.

VI. Another Incident at St. Mark's

The red haired priest pulled on the door at the very center of the great church. Slowly it responded to his efforts. A stiff breeze was blowing increasing the difficulty of moving its great weight. The door separated two worlds. On the inside, it protected a place of reverence and holiness. On the outside, it offered these holy qualities to a city known for glamour and excitement. However, it did not divide the opulence of both the church and the city.

Antonio Vivaldi

As the great portal opened, the priest caught a glimpse of the overwhelming magnificence of the cathedral. The massive space, the ornate altar, the fantastic paintings; all were meant to overpower the worshipper. He now felt its power. A trembling of excitement flooded over him. His heartbeat increased. His pulse quickened.

He glanced over his shoulder to view the most sensational city in Europe. Venice was alive with musicians, singers, markets, lagoons, gondolas and gondoliers. It was good to be home again, he thought.

A traveler appeared. The priest held the door for the gentleman. He inquired, "First time to St. Mark's Cathedral?"

"It is," came the reply.

The priest noted the dress of a foreigner. Probably hails from the Lowlands he guessed.

"Have you traveled far?" he asked the stranger.

"From Amsterdam."

The priest had surmised correctly. Tourists from the Low Countries were frequent visitors to Venice. "We see many Netherlanders here. Speaking for myself, I appreciate your great city of Amsterdam."

"And why is that?"

"All Venetians love the money you bring," he said in a joking fashion. More seriously, he continued, "Several of my compositions have been published in your great city."

A sharp gust pressed hard on the opened door. The immense weight of it and the intensity of the breeze shifted directly against the priest. The effort to sustain its heft caused him to cough sharply and repeatedly. He let the door go. It closed with a disturbing bang. The two were left outdoors in the stiff winds.

Posing his question with some hesitance, the traveler asked, "So you are a composer?" He hoped he had not embarrassed himself. Perhaps, he thought the question might be a bit impertinent.

The priest answered quickly and with delight. "A composer *and* a priest." Then he added in a quieter tone, "I much prefer music to the priesthood."

"And why is that?"

"I never enjoyed being a priest."

"Why then did you study for the clergy?"

"Out of necessity. My family was poor. In fact, my father was a barber. He said that if I trained for the priesthood, I could be schooled at no cost. I was drawn into the priesthood because of my education."

Again the priest coughed. This second outburst lasted for a considerable number of seconds. Pointing to his chest, "In fact, I suffer from a tightness in the chest which has caused a breathing problem. I've had this since I was a boy. With such a limitation in my lungs, it became difficult to perform Holy Mass. One year after my ordination I was given a reprieve from celebrating the Eucharist, all due to the illness."

"Are you now active as a priest?"

"No. I remain a priest but do not practice as a clergyman."

The priest did not want to carry this discussion any further. He changed the subject. "Tell me, my good friend, are you a communicant of the Catholic faith?"

"No, I am of a more liberal mind. My visit to St.

Mark's is to see its beauty and its oriental design."

The casualness of the man's remark smacked at Vivaldi's heart. He drew back ever so slightly. "Probably a radical protestant," Vivaldi thought, "Amsterdam is full of them."

"The magnificence of St. Mark's exterior is breathtaking. I am eager to see its interior." After a moment, he smiled, extended his right arm and pronounced, "My name is Jan van York, banker and trader of woolen goods."

"I am Antonio Vivaldi, priest , composer, violinist and teacher."

Van York asked, "You seem quite at home here. Are you, indeed, from here in Venice?"

"I *was* from Venice." Vivaldi told him.

"Please explain," Van York said, eager to hear about a man who had music published all the way in Amsterdam.

"I have been away for many years. Many travels. Many appointments. I am now returning to Venice. I only arrived yesterday from Rome. I spent three years there."

"Venice is quite a change from Rome, I would assume," remarked van York.

"A great deal more secular here," motioning toward the city.

A few perfunctory remarks followed. Both decided to shrug off the impious nature of Venice and move into the sacredness of St. Mark's. Van York took charge of opening the great portal. Both men entered the sanctity before them.

The cavernous spaces of St. Mark's thrilled both men. It wasn't just the space, it was the resonance of its walls. Jan van York was taken by the six-and-a-half second reverberation. Even the most breathless of sounds echoed repeatedly in its chambers. They could hear hushed whispers, the shuffle of feet, the rustling of clothes and calm words intoned by the priest. Each echo evaporated into nothingness.

Suddenly a new sound emerged. It was coming from one of the organ lofts. Softly bathing the listener in a series of heavenly and sonorous harmonies came the echoes of pipes enclosed in the swell division of the pipe organ. They filled the room.

Van York, an amateur musician himself, took note of the music. It had a simple texture. Its melodious nature seemed far less complex than the music Van York had heard in the Low Countries. He was enraptured.

Vivaldi did not share the joy of his new acquaintance. A scowl was forming over his face. Beginning below his ears, then flowing upward along each cheek was a developing pink shade. It then turned red and grew brighter until his forehead matched the crimson shade of his hair. Vivaldi was about to explode. Van York feared words would fly. They did.

"How can the organ be so out of tune!" It was whispered, but it carried the intensity of a volcano.

Visitors and communicants shot looks toward the two. Van York looked away hoping he would not be blamed for such outrageous behavior.

Vivaldi, on the other hand, took some enjoyment in the situation. He glanced about the nave. One couple was laughing. An old man stared in disgust. Most however, simply looked away, pretending it had not happened, not in the sanctity of this holy place.

Vivaldi said it again, "How can the organ be so out of tune?" This time his voice went beyond a whisper. "I tell you the flute rank is out of tune with the strings. What fool would allow an ill-tuned organ to be played for Matins service?"

There. He'd said it. There was nothing more to say. He had made his complaint. The subject was dropped.

Had he been asked, Vivaldi would have admitted the intonation was not as awful as he had made it seem. He simply was disappointed that after fourteen years, he wanted his return to Venice to be perfect. It had gotten off to a poor start.

Vivaldi restrained himself. He took a deep breath, hoping to avoid another coughing attack and got his temper under control. Such wretched outbursts were not unusual for him. His emotions were mercurial, rising quickly, then vanishing with similar haste.

Letting the organ issue die, Vivaldi moved to the altar to receive the Eucharist. He took his place at the bench and knelt in reverence. He could see the approaching figure of the priest who had already begun speaking the words of the Holy Feast. Words of the Mass were growing louder as the priest came his way. As he knelt, Vivaldi's mind took leave from St. Mark's. A series of images formed; a warm spring day, the rawness of a winter's storm, the heat of summer. All these passed through his mind in an instant. His thoughts, however, had not impeded the progress of the priest. His words were growing louder, ever clearer, but Vivaldi never heard them. He never processed them within his consciousness.

The priest gave the sign of the cross and with reverence spoke, "*Domine Deus.*" They fell in a vacuum. Vivaldi's mind was a dizzying flood of fresh new melodies. A parade of lovely airs and beautiful melodies was coursing his thinking. It wasn't just the music that was fresh. A whole new idea was formulating. It was a vision of something new and different.

Why had it happened precisely at this moment? What had caused this thought that pierced his consciousness? Possibly, he thought, it had been the liveliness of the city that had hit him in a strange and miraculous way. Impulses took over him.

Fancies captured his mind. The priest now stood directly in front of him, but his words were lost by the impulses and fancies. The Holy Elements were now right before him. The Very Body of the Savior. He looked up to receive them.

Suddenly, he was gone. Vivaldi simply stood up and left. Not a word. Not a sign of the peace. Not a humble bow of thanks. Nothing. Simply, up and gone.

Vivaldi was both an impulsive man and an expeditious composer. As a man, he could be expected to act in thoughtless ways. He had shown extreme behavior in the past. His temper matched his hair, red and fiery. As a composer, no one could match his pace for speed. His reputation for turning out music at a hectic pace was legendary. He bragged he could write music faster than his copyists could copy it. A German musician once asked if he could write a concerto. Three days later, Vivaldi handed him ten; all new works. This sudden and impulsive departure from St. Mark's was all within his character.

Within a week of the St. Mark's episode, Vivaldi settled into his studio. Several ongoing commission projects kept him busy and happy. Each month he wrote two concertos for the girls at the *Ospedale della Pieta.* His mind flashed back to his first day at the *Ospedale.*

"Welcome to our orphanage, Senor Vivaldi," the nun said. "I am Sister Anna."

"A well-seasoned Sister Anna," thought Vivaldi, noting the wrinkles crisscrossing her face.

She continued her welcome. "Although you are still young yourself, you have been highly recommended as a teacher of violin. You have been hired because the gentlemen of Venice want only the finest education for the girls they have entreated to our care."

"Young?" he responded. "The year is 1703, I am already twenty-five years of age. I am probably ten years older than most of the girls."

With a gentle nod, Sister Anna dismissed his protest. "I only say such because many of our girls have never met their mothers. Most are orphans. The men of Venice, many of them with significant power, feel a responsibility to the young ladies."

"I will do my part," Vivaldi reassured her. She showed him to his teaching studio.

It took very little time for Vivaldi to find teaching at the *Ospedale* an enjoyable experience. The girls were bright. Many of them were already excellent musicians. They played the violin, cello, flute, oboe and bassoon. Their performances were a frequent delight to audiences of Venice. The girls of the school became an inspiration to him. Floods of exercises and etudes poured from him. Solo pieces. Works for string orchestra. Shelves were filling with his suites and concertos. Especially concertos.

"Ladies," he would say, "I have thoughts for a new concerto. Who would like to the be the soloist?"

Hands would fly up. Promises of practicing more hours were made, and sometimes kept. A day or two later, Vivaldi would have the work in his hands. Eager fingers waited to bring his creation to life.

Vivaldi found the concerto the perfect form. It allowed him all the freedom he needed both as a composer and a teacher. His concertos inspired the girls. The competition it bred improved the standards of their performances.

The concerto was not a new idea. Composers had been composing them for years. Vivaldi gave the concerto a whole new level of distinction. With blazing speed, he would select an instrument and write music perfectly suited for it. It was a complement of player and instrument. Each concerto had three contrasting sections, called movements. Each movement was a complete piece of music. It was ordered in a "fast—slow—fast" format, from which he rarely departed.

The music was a reflection of who he was. His music was like his personality: mercurial, passionate, quick, and most of all, not given to pretences. Seldom did he waver from a first movement that was a display of rapid scales, lively melodies, decorations of trills and embellishments. The girls loved them. He gave them ample opportunity to show off their virtuoso qualities.

Vivaldi often reminded them that music that was fast could hide some deficiencies. "A flurry of notes dashed off carelessly only makes a bad musician grow worse," he would tell his classes.

Determined to open their musical souls, Vivaldi created second movements that moved the spirit. Moving at a purposeful slower tempo, Vivaldi's creations were built on rich emotions, drawn-out phrases and pleasant melodies which often evoked a tear or two from one of the ladies of the audience. The girls took great delight when a tear was shed. With a delightful release of tension, a finale of dazzling display rounded out each concerto. Ten minutes of delight and it was over. He created hundreds of them for his students.

His return to Venice was prompted by opera. It was the rage of the city. Audiences gravitated to it like dogs to fresh meat. They simply could not get enough opera. They wanted new operas. New arias. New and fresh music. Who better than Vivaldi with his quick pen to meet their demands? He committed himself to composing four operas in his first year there.

Still, Vivaldi could not put down the novel idea formulated at St. Mark's a week earlier. His mind was bubbling with an idea for a collection of concertos that went beyond mere musical creations.

"I am thinking of creating a great concerto based on the elements of nature," he told one of his former students who had come to pay him a visit. It was Maria. She was eager to see him after all these years. He hardly recognized her.

"Senor Vivaldi, I remember singing many an air you composed that quoted the coos of the dove, or quoted the hunter's songs. I think your idea of a work based on nature is a grand one."

"No, no, no," Vivaldi could see she was missing the point. "I mean more than merely quoting some hunter's melody, or the bellow of some bull, I mean to capture the essence of nature itself."

She could not catch his visions. She did, however, understand the wealth of his talents. "Master," she said, "you can do anything you dream. I know it."

Her words were like a challenge to him. She departed, he imparted. His thoughts took root.

Vivaldi began by creating four sonnets, each a visualization of the delights of each season. He entitled the work *Four Seasons*. He set out to compose a series of concertos expressing the essences of spring, summer, autumn and winter. He composed words that conjured up images.

"Springtime is upon us. The birds celebrate her return with festive song, and murmuring streams are softly caressed by the breezes. Thunderstorms, those heralds of spring, roar, casting their dark mantle over heaven…"

Then on to summer.

"Beneath the blazing sun's relentless heat men and flocks are sweltering, pines are scored." The music blazed with the intensity of blistering afternoons.

Vivaldi's third sonnet celebrated the joys of autumn.

"The peasant celebrates with song and dance the harvest safely gathered in." Within its movements he slowed to express "the cooling breezes fan the pleasant air, inviting all to sleep without a care."

Vivaldi plunged forward to the stinging sensation of winter's chill. Intense music to express the "shivering, frozen mid the frosty snow in biting, stinging winds." Calm melodies to accompany those who "rest contentedly beside the hearth."

A marvelous transcription of words became music. Letters became notes. Sentences became melodies.

Vivaldi's *Four Seasons* streamed forth effortlessly, skillfully and passionately. At breakneck speed the images took musical shape. He gave no thought of the morrow. He was expressing himself in the moment. Vivaldi composed for his own joy. He was not driven by fame or fortune. He would say, "A hundred years from now who would ever care?"

The thought never bothered him.

Author's note: Jan van York and Sister Anna were fictitious persons.

VIII. Incident at Leipzig

"Herr Sebastian Bach, we find ourselves at odds again. Your stubborn nature has put our Council in an awkward and difficult position."

The words were spoken by the Council President of the City of Leipzig. Leipzig was a significantly large municipality of 30,000 people located in the northern regions of Germany. Leipzig was also home to the Church of St. Thomas, an important center of Lutheranism. On this particular afternoon in 1732, the Council was meeting with Johann Sebastian Bach, a composer of considerable fame. He was employed as the Cantor of St. Thomas Church. As such, he was the organist, composer, as well as teacher at the school associated with the church. The appointment as Cantor was not an insignificant one. The Cantor of St. Thomas was a prestigious position in an important city.

Johann Sebastian Bach

As Cantor, Bach answered to the Council. He had been asked to appear before the governing group and he was not happy. Neither was this the first time he had aired his grievances. A degree of some animosity had developed between him and the Council.

Johann Sebastian began. "Herr Council President, with all respect as a servant to you and the church, I have a few concerns, or perhaps I should call them grievances, to bring before you today. They concern promises made, but promises not kept. I remind the Council that many assurances were made when I arrived five years ago. Many of these have been left unfulfilled."

Of the Council members, Walter Muller was the most distrustful toward Bach. He fired back. "Sir," spoken in a derisive manner, "which promise do you say the Council has not fulfilled?"

The question touched a sensitive nerve of the composer. "Most upsetting is the salary of 1,000 talers per year promised to me by Gottlieb Manor. As you will recall, he was Mayor at the time.

Council President Wilhelm Gratz, the man most sympathetic to Bach, tried to defuse the issue. In a tone of reasonable temper, he asked the composer, "Herr Bach, do we not pay you an ample salary? Do you wish to compare your yearly stipend with those of persons in similar positions in other communities? I think you will find that the Council pays quite handsomely."

The other members nodded in agreement. Some members more than nodded, they raised their eyebrows with an arrogance that indicated how impressed they were with themselves by their own generosity.

Had he been pushed quietly, Bach would have admitted that his salary was more than ample. He was making a decent living. He was, however, bothered by their lack of principles;

that they would deny a promise made to him by the mayor.

The salary issue was concern enough. Another anxiety bothered him even more. It affected his family. Sebastian was disturbed by the appalling apartment the family had been given to live in. The living conditions the church provided were deplorable. As the protector of his family, Bach was not a man to back down.

With his face burning in passion, he spoke to each Council member in succession. Staring directly into their eyes, he nearly shouted. "If money were the only thing, I could accept it. My concern is for my loved ones. My family is aggrieved by your inconsiderate attitude toward their well being."

However, his powerful words did not fall on sensitive ears.

Councilman Thomas Schmidt interrupted, "We are most generous men. Have we not provided an apartment for you? What right have you to complain?"

Bach's nerves were set on fire. "Apartment? Apartment? Sure, an apartment, if that's what you want to call a place filled with vermin of all types. The place is overrun by rats and mice. The conditions are deplorable. It is harshly cold and drafty in the winter. The place is ruled more by bugs and insects than by humans. It is an unhealthy and unfit place for any man to raise his family."

Several members scoffed at these outlandish claims. Councilman Leopold Korngold shot back, "Unhealthy? It is a ridiculous claim! How can you make it?"

Bach lowered his voice to a whisper, but the words were delivered with vengeance. "Sirs, of the children born in my years at Leipzig, all but one has died as a child." He raised his voice. "Can you imagine the grief this has caused me and my dear wife Anna Magdalena?"

The comment softened the men of the Council. Like the Cantor, they too had suffered the loss of children.

After a few moments of tension-filled silence, Councilman Herrmann Goltmann tried to set the conversation on better grounds. He began, "The apartment is cold in winter. I will grant you that. What other apartment in Leipzig isn't cold in the winter? And the rats? Well, I don't like them either. But rats are a part of life. They will always run loose." Goltmann hesitated, then asked. "And what else do you propose we do for you and your family?"

Bach now moved to the heart of his complaints. "The apartment is directly adjacent to the boy's school. The school is overrun with ruffians. Fifty of them. Fifty rowdy ruffians—and that's what they are—can make quite a racket! With a half dozen of my own children living in my house, and my work as a composer, I need a place of quiet. The noise of the boys is overwhelming. There is but a thin partition between my family and these hooligans."

Council President asked, "And what is it you request?"

Bach responded, "I implore you to improve the health of the building. Provide at least a wall, not a mere partition between the school and my apartment. These are small requests given the importance of the position I hold."

The Council members looked at each other. A moment later, Council President Gratz said, "Before we consider your request, some Council members feel it necessary to review your personal file. Your record indicates a few problems in the past. When you arrived here at St. Thomas School five years ago in 1727, these personal issues gave us reservations. We agreed you were an exceptionally fine composer and without doubt, the finest organist in all of Germany. But your record is blemished. Let me review a few cases. In Lubeck you were involved in a serious brawl with a man named Geyersbach. I believe you even drew your sword."

"The account is true. I was but eighteen at the time. Young, impetuous and impulsive."

"Explain yourself," demanded Councilman Schmidt.

Bach was more than happy to give his side of the story.

"Geyersbach was a horrid musician. The man was a wretched fool. He attempted to play the bassoon but it sounded like the groans of a goat. I told him so. He attacked me. I drew my sword. I did so to protect the honor of music itself."

Councilman Goltmann noted, "I also see that you received a severe reprimand from your employer. You acted in an insubordinate way without regard to your superiors. It was when you had requested a leave of one month. You were gone six. Explain that."

"I had walked 250 miles to hear the great organist Buxtehude. I was so enthralled I could not return without gaining all I could from his musical wisdom."

"I believe this bordered on insubordination!" commented Councilman Thomas Benz.

The inquiry was not over. Council President Gratz recalled another incident. "Were you not put in jail for nearly a month in Weimar?"

Sebastian pleaded, "Again, it was a misunderstanding. I had upset the Duke of Weimar because I wanted to leave for a better position. In fact I forced the issue of leaving. He wanted to deny me the privilege. I objected. My objections got out of hand— even I admit that. The Duke put me under house arrest, but I was released after three weeks."

The meeting put both the composer and the Council in foul moods. All was not lost. Council President Gratz felt it was time to change the mood of the session.

"Gentlemen of the Council," he began, "I think we can agree that Johann Sebastian has a few blemishes. In truth, don't we all? I think we must overlook any personal differences we have with the man. Undeniably, he has served us well. Beyond well. He has served us exceedingly well. When he came to us, he was our third choice. Yet, look what this man does. He works incessantly. He provides a cantata nearly every Sunday. Gentleman, do I have to remind you that his cantatas are twenty minutes long? Think of the time to merely pen the notes. Putting hundreds of notes and notations in scores requires hours upon hours. In addition, he has given us score upon score of organ works. I will add that these are great organ works."

Councilman Schmidt interrupted, "Great!! If by the word *great,* you mean long. Yes he gives us excessively *great* works."

Councilman Goltmann added, "Many times we have expressed our displeasure at the great length of his works. Does he shorten them? No! On other occasions, he makes them so short, they leave gaps in the service. I tell you, the man is incorrigible."

"Gentlemen, gentlemen," Gratz said, trying to calm them both, "as I was saying, he has given us organ works, preludes and fugues for the clavier, suites for the violin, oboe and other instruments. And every Friday evening, he provides music for the Neal Coffeehouses."

Councilman Wolff, Bach's deepest admirer, added in a complimentary gesture, "I would add that his compositions are works of the highest order, though I must admit I do not understand them. On occasion they became too lengthy, too complex, and they rarely present a melody that could be sung with ease. Yet, I have no doubt, Bach is among the most able of all German composers."

President Gratz continued, "Councilman, I believe Herr Bach is an honorable man with reasonable concerns. We shall take up these matters for discussion."

Johann Sebastian moved on to another frustration that had become a source of great aggravation. It was focused on the cantankerous nature of the youngsters of the school.

"Men of the Council," Bach began, "what can be done about the boys of the school? Disciplining them is near to impossible. Many come from broken homes. They lack proper upbringing and act in delinquent ways. If that weren't bad enough, their musical abilities seriously hamper my abilities to produce a favorable concert. Some are good musicians. Many, though, can barely match a pitch. The rest are hopeless. Frankly, they are tone deaf. How can I produce a quality performance with such a mix-matched ensemble?"

Council President Gratz told him, "I speak for the entire Council when I say that we respect your great musical instincts. However, it is the mission of St. Thomas Church, this Council and the City of Leipzig to educate these boys. Your duty is to instill music in them as part of their education. These young men come to you with whatever musical skills God has given them. We can do nothing about what God has granted. Therefore, if the boys do not come up to your musical standards, you will have to compromise your writing to suit their abilities."

"Compromise!" The word shot Bach into a rage. "I do not lower my standards. Under no circumstance do I made concessions to the art of music. My life and my composing are to honor God. I compose to the glory of the one God. I will do no less. I absolutely refuse to compromise."

With that, he tore himself from the meeting. Five minutes later, he arrived home in a most unpleasant temper. The door shot open.

Sebastian stepped across the threshold. "The Council has done it again!" His words bordered on shouting.

The room went silent.

"What is it, Dear?" asked Anna Magdalena.

"They have asked me to compromise my music!" He flung his coat on the table. "Then they complain my works are too long. Or too short." He stopped, motioned with his arm around the room. "That's not all, they offer no hope or help in improving this apartment."

Anna Magdalena crossed the room, took Sebastian in her arms and gave him a gentle kiss on the cheek. She loved her husband deeply and worshipped his music. Fortunately for him, she could also calm him down. Anna Magdalena was the partner he so desperately needed.

In her persuading way, she said, "Perhaps after dinner we can discuss this. The boys are working hard for you, let's not disturb them right now."

Anna Magdalena had spent the afternoon guiding the two eldest sons, Carl Phillip Emmanuel and Wilhelm Friedmann. It was their duty to copy the music their father had written. They were skillful workers and used the duties to develop their own strong skills as composers. The other children were focused on music lessons or practicing their instruments. Everyone was thoroughly occupied. Their father's outburst had shaken them initially, but now they had returned to their tasks. Sebastian's belligerent entry had also disturbed Anna who had been practicing the harpsichord pieces her husband had written specifically for her.

Johann Sebastian took a quick look around at the children. The sight of them calmed his nerves. He plopped himself into a chair. His eyes fell on a musical score of Vivaldi. He picked it up. In a moment, he was looking at each note of every page. He was soon absorbed in the music, learning from it, educating himself in the Italian style. It gave him great joy. He forgot about the Council. He let go his concerns about the boys. Here at home he wrapped himself in the joys of family and music. They were all that he needed.

An hour later dinner was completed. Anna suggested the whole family gather around the harpsichord and set about for an evening of singing and playing musical games. She didn't have to ask twice. The family loved and excelled at anything musical. Sounds of joy, singing, excitement rang out through the apartment.

Then a knock on the front door was heard. It was Council President Gratz. "I have come to tell you, my good friend Sebastian, the Council has heard your concerns. They voted in unanimous accord to make all the upgrades in the apartment that you and your family need. Their questions meant no harm or ill. We are honored to have you as part of St. Thomas. We intend to keep you on our staff for many, many years."

Sebastian accepted the good favors of the Council. It sent him into excited spirits. He turned to Carl Phillip and demanded as a challenge, "Hum for me, my son, a short tune that I can improvise as a fugue."

The opportunity ignited a smile on Carl's face. In a moment, he had thought out a short melody. He sang it.

"Excellent, my son," granted Sebastian. He moved directly to the harpsichord. Without a moment's hesitation, the tune was turned into a fugue of three voices. Minutes later the old man was digging further into the implications of Carl's tune. He turned it upside down, even played it backward. The whole family was entranced. Smiles abounded. The apartment shook with laughs and shouts of joy. Music crowned the evening, as it had done so many times before. Surely more days like it would follow.

Author's note: The members of the Church Council were fictitious including, President Wilhelm Gratz and members Walter Muller, Leopold Korngold, Thomas Schmidt, Herrmann Goltmann, Frederick Wolff and Thomas Benz.

IX. Incident at Dublin, Ireland

It was an excitement that sprang like a tiger from a box. It was uncontrollable and irrepressible. The people of Dublin, Ireland were caught in an exhilaration unlike anything they had ever experienced. Like a raging wildfire word was spreading that the greatest musical event, not just of the year—but possibly the greatest musical event ever—was about to take place. In just four days.

George Frederich Handel

The mania was unleashed on one particular day in April, 1742. In actuality the process had begun several weeks earlier in rehearsals for the great unveiling. It was on that April 9th that the public was treated to the first airing of a new and great work for chorus, singers and orchestra. The work was an oratorio with the title *Messiah*. The composer was a man with a reputation of legendary proportions, George Frederick Handel. Besides being an excellent composer, he was friend of the King of England, champion of the middle class and a smart business-man. He was also capable of transporting audiences to spec-tacular heights. (For the time being, we shall overlook that he was overweight, ate too much, was unfaithful to any kind of physical activity, possessed with odd work habits and was one who failed to temper his own temper.) On those early spring days of 1742, he was a musical hero to Dublin. That was all that mattered to the city.

Handel was on an extended visit to Dublin, on leave from his hometown of London. The British capital was not truly his home, rather it was the adopted abode of the German-born composer. That didn't matter to the British. For decades, Britons had accepted Handel as one of their own. They thrilled to his music and flocked to his concerts. That is, they came as long as he composed to their fickle tastes.

Handel took a short leave of England to stay in Dublin at the invitation of the viceroy of the city. The two had agreed to provide a series of concerts of Handel's music as a charity performance. A portion of the profits of his concerts would be devoted to a local hospital in need of funds.

Years later Handel would conduct performances of *Messiah* to offer hope to debtors unable to raise the funds they needed to release them from prison. On an occasion or two, debtor's prison was something Handel had come desperately close to experiencing himself. Although he was a fine and clever businessman, he had had a few close calls with imprison-ment over unpaid debts. He understood the importance of his charitable act.

From the 9th of April till the 13th of the month, Dublin went mad. The first airing was a clever gimmick intended to guarantee an audience. It prompted people to spread words of praise and heightened anticipation that bordered on a frenzy. Tickets were hard to come by. The people's words were matched by the marketing skills of Handel. He put out notices in the papers. He called for public rehearsals where people could sit, hear, and enjoy the makings of the piece without paying a penny. He welcomed them knowing they would carry the word of this majestic piece to others. They proclaimed *Messiah* to be a masterpiece before it was ever performed.

These final days before the premiere were nerve-wrenching, hectic days for Handel. Every passing hour was consumed with frenzied activities, none of them the same. He worked at a dizzying pace making last-minute changes to the music. There were arias to be rewritten. It wasn't that the music was not satisfactory, but as Handel heard each particular singer perform his music, he decided on changes. He altered passages to suit the abilities of each singer. It was a massive undertaking and a risky one as well. The new music had to be recopied, re-learned, then rehearsed again. Time was crowding in. The premiere was but a day or two away. He touched up portions of the score. In some cases, he dumped the original music and inserted pieces from other works, some of it may not have been his own. What did that matter? The success, the enormous success, of the anticipated performance was all that mattered.

Then there were matters of spreading the word. Handel ordered the publicity mills into action. Each hour he was pressed for last-minute details of the theater, including lighting and staging. Handel found himself settling squabbles among the singers, correcting errors committed by the copyists and answering endless logistical questions. Fortunate for him, Handel was a man used to such tensions. As an impresario in London for years, he had done it all. Composer. Arranger. Marketer. Publicist. Manager. Advisor. Mediator. These were all old hat to him. However these activities had often tested his temper and drove him into fits of rage. He was known as a man who could not easily control his anxieties. He strove to squelch his outbursts at this historic moment.

The great premiere came on the night of April 13. The audience was caught in delirious excitement. Over the next two to three hours they would experience a work of art that was a lifetime in making. In *Messiah* was encapsulated the fruits, joys, pains, depression, mania, thrills and depths of Handel's own life.

The piece itself was composed within a unique set of circumstances where fact and fiction had been so firmly intertwined that the real truth was obscured. *Messiah* had been formulating in his mind over the course of several years. However, Handel actually began work on *Messiah* on August 22, 1741. He envisioned a work of exceptional length. It was to be long and thorough, a work of biblical proportions and underpinnings, but intended for performances in concert halls. The text had been suggested by Charles Jennens who took passages from the scriptures to portray the life of Christ, the Messiah. To compose the work, Handel would require quiet, separation and seclusion.

Handel settled into a small cottage on the Jennens estate. The seed of *Messiah* had been planted years ago. He cultivated it in his mind, whether in hours of awakening or in the depths of great sleep. At times it pervaded his thinking. Other times it slipped back into unconscious oblivion. Yet it developed. From a seed, to a root, to a plant, to a bud. By the time it had reached the point of blossom, he had worked himself into a manic state. It overtook him. It demanded complete and unequivocal concentration. He gave in to its power.

Messiah had now put him in a condition of mania. His mind was working at peak performance. His brain was a series of nerves and neurons firing at a blistering, unending pace. They were connecting ideas, pulling the experience of his fifty-seven years into full action. He was intense. He was agitated.

Handel had had experience with these periods of mania in the past. He knew what to expect. He could work endlessly without ceasing. He would not give in to exhaustion. Days and nights were mixed up in a confusion of turmoil. The body separated from the mind. He could go on without sleep, stretch the hours between meals, lock himself up into seclusion and push himself beyond the limits of human endurance. He had done it before, he could do it once again.

From August 22 until September 15 he worked his pen until his fingers could no longer carry the weight of the pen. The tedium of twenty-four days produced pages and pages of musical scores. They brought forth notes in the tens of thousands focused on one great task. A work worthy of God Almighty. He worked feverishly, like a man mad with inspiration.

Handel's work was a conglomeration of all-new pieces for the chorus. In addition to music for chorus, lyric arias would be composed for the four classes of voices. There would be the lyricism of the soprano, the heftiness of the alto, the lightness of the tenor and the strength of the bass. One by one they would be woven together in one spiritual act of praise and honor. Handel was well skilled in composing for voice which was built on years of composing operas with brilliant arias devoted to the solo voices. Each aria and chorus was a work of art in itself. Now his great oratorio, *Messiah*, required the stringing together of forty-one separate and magnificent pieces into one large work. Each movement served as a piece of a gigantic puzzle creating an image of the Son of God. If one aria or chorus were substandard, the entire work would suffer miserably.

He labored through hours which grew to days, then slipped into weeks. He ordered his servants to leave him alone, to bring his meals only when he requested. Working himself to delirium, he would rest for a few hours, eat a small meal, then return to his work.

Then it happened.

He was struck with one word. One powerful term that expressed the joy of life. One overwhelming expression that left him awestruck. "Hallelujah!"

"Hallelujah!" He turned the word over and over again in his head. He envisioned its true meaning. He uttered it repeatedly while feeling its rhythm, its life, its cadence. Ha. Le. Lu. Jah. Four syllables united as one. He pounced on the first syllable, lengthened it to double— even triple the value of the remaining three. The word took musical shape as he placed 'Ha' higher by several pitches than the others. Then he extracted 'Lu' making it the focus of the accent. The exclamation became ha-a-a -a le LU jah. He said it again, then selected the correct notes to heighten the impact of the word. He repeated the joyous word again and again. Inspiration descended on him. He flew into the work full force. For the next hour he gloriously transformed the word Hallelujah into a musical masterpiece. The words "He shall reign forever and ever" were added to intensify the joy of each succeeding "Hallelujah."

As he closed in on the final and glorious "Hallelujah," a vision appeared before him. It was an image created in his state of ecstasy, a revelation to match that of St. John's. His head fell into his arms. Great tears of joy grew into sobs of praise and adoration. The commotion attracted the attention of his servant who rushed into the room.

With tears streaming down his cheeks, Handel confessed, "I did think I did see all Heaven before me, and the great God Himself."

Several days later, he jotted down the ultimate "Amen." *Messiah* was completed in just twenty-four days. In merely three and half weeks, one of music's greatest masterpieces was completed.

Though it was finished, *Messiah* left him with a dilemma. Where might it be performed? Two options were available. The church was most obvious. Yet, the work was too closely related to opera, a genre of the secular world It begged the question; was it acceptable for performance in an ecclesiastical setting? The concert hall was a second option, but that too posed difficulties. Its biblical text posed a barrier. Many would be shocked by a scriptural work in a venue outside of the church. Cries of sacrilege were certain to be cast about.

For months, Handel held on to the great work, waiting for just the right moment to unveil *Messiah*. That momentous occasion came when Lord Lieutenant of Dublin contracted the composer to give a series of concerts to benefit a local charity. Handel gathered several of his most popular works to precede the premiere of *Messiah*. At each concert, his fame and reputation grew throughout Dublin. As April approached, the anticipation of its residents grew. The final days leading to the premiere witnessed a flurry of heightened anticipation.

On April 13, 1742 Neal's Music Hall on Fishamble Street was jammed. Every seat had been taken. The women had been forewarned not to wear their hooped skirts. They took up too much room. Men were told not to wear their swords. Like the skirts, the swords assumed greater breadth and swallowed up valuable space. Hundreds of people were unable to get in the hall. They listened through doors and windows. The music left them smitten in awe. It was a momentous night that elevated the reputation of Handel to untold heights.

A year later *Messiah* received a second performance. The London audience, too, caught the excitement, though it was more tempered than the Dublin crowd. King George was in attendance. He caused a unique tradition to begin. When the glorious chorus "Hallelujah" was sung, the power and drama of the music so overwhelmed him that he rose to his feet. When the king stood, the people, too, were obliged to stand. King George stood because of the music. The audience stood because King George stood. A tradition was born. Even today when "Hallelujah" is sung, audiences stand.

It is a grand tradition three hundred years old.

X. Incident at London, England

Franz Joseph Haydn put down his pen and closed the musical score he had spent the better part of the day working on. He was exhausted from a six-hour stretch of composing. His shoulders and back were weary. Every muscle ached. His mind was numb and his fingers ached from the strain of creating original music then writing it down on paper exactly as he had heard it. Rubbing his eyes, he stood, gained his balance, then focused his tired eyes back on the great work he had been writing. It wasn't finished, but already it was the size of a large book. He picked up the score. It contained his new symphony, the 94th. Ninety-four! He thought about that for just a moment. 94 symphonies! It was, by any count, an incredible number. There were so many that even he wasn't sure of the number.

Franz Joseph Haydn

Though at least ninety-three symphonies had preceded this one, Haydn was taking nothing for granted. He lavished considerable attention and time on this work. He was intent on producing a work that was worthy of his excellent and widespread reputation. In 1790, Haydn was considered one of the finest composers in all of Germany and Austria. Considering that these were the most important musical centers of the age, that made him among the finest composers in all of Europe. Even with such a distinguished reputation he remained a humble man, though confident in himself.

He opened the score. The title page bore his name, the number of the symphony, 94, and that it was scored in G Major. It also included an inscription that read that the symphony was commissioned by J. P. Salomon of London, England.

He leafed through its pages. It was full of tunes that were pleasant, upbeat and buoyant. Soon he was singing the main themes. His head began moving in time with the music, while his fingers tapped lightly on his chest, outlining the shape of the tuneful melodies. His thoughts brought on several nods of approval, and one tune actually caused a splendid smile to form on his face.

After a few more moments, Haydn set the score back on the piano rack and sat down for a cup of tea. The rest gave him opportunity to dream. His reverie took him to the night when the symphony was to be premiered. He could see it all. If J. P. Salomon was right, London would be all abuzz with large crowds. Certainly, Haydn thought, Salomon, if anyone, would be able to predict such things. He was an impresario, a man who could make others famous while lining his own pockets. It made for two happy people. Salomon explained that women would be outfitted in elegant gowns. They would come bedecked in jewelry while the gentlemen would be attired in distinguished suits, topped with expensive hats that proved their self-importance. They would come to hear his new symphony.

When Salomon first approached Haydn, he explained that England longed for a great composer. Since George Frederick Handel had died some thirty-five years earlier, the city languished for a composer of substance. The country had rarely produced a composer worthy of those from the German states, France, Austria or Italy, the other leading musical centers.

Not only were large audiences anticipated, there were generous profits to be made. Londoners were ready to pay good money for music that was worth the price of admission. Haydn was sure his symphony would attract them.

On New Year's Day in 1791, Haydn arrived in England's largest city. He was overwhelmed by his hero's welcome. He was quite surprised to discover that he was famous. He had no idea that his fame had crossed the English Channel where the British acclaimed him as worthy a composer as Handel. He spent a wonderful year and a half on the British Isles. While in London, he spent nearly every day composing, attending lavish parties, composing, feasting on sumptuous banquets, composing, accepting adoring visitors and composing. Mostly, he composed.

Although Haydn had agreed to compose a number of new symphonies for the London audiences, he was greatly concerned that this one, the 94th, would set a bar of excellence. It must be his best writing. He was certain he was not to be outdone by his cross-town rival, Pleyel. Of this symphony there must be something special. It simply had to have a unique feature that would set it apart from the others, even from his own works.

Haydn had two remarkable commodities that enabled him to complete an excellent symphony like the 94th in a relatively short span of time. He had been writing symphonies for thirty years and he possessed a great work ethic based on consistent work day after day.

The lion's share of his career had been spent working in the court of Prince Esterhazy. The Esterhazy estate was an immense and lavish palace that was second in size and opulence only to Versailles, built just outside Paris by King Louis

XVI. Prince Esterhazy employed a small, but excellent orchestra on a full-time basis. He was a lover of great music and offered regular concerts to visiting kings, queens, and other members of royalty. He insisted on excellence.

To compose music for his esteemed ensemble, the Prince had selected Haydn to be his court composer in 1761. It was a successful arrangement for all. Esterhazy had great affection for Haydn's music. The musicians appreciated Haydn's cheerful outlook on life and the music he wrote was superb. Oftentimes, the composer wrote specific passages for selected players in the orchestra giving them ample opportunity to portray their individual skills. Completing the pleasantness among the prince and his musicians was Haydn's willingness to accept himself as a servant. Socially, he understood that he was to eat with the servants, and was to be housed in private quarters placed in the vicinity alongside the other servant's housing. Of all the servants, he held the highest position, yet was amply satisfied in his role.

For the next twenty-nine years Haydn served Prince Esterhazy faithfully. The Prince died in 1790 much to the dismay of everyone who knew and served him. Then his brother assumed control. He did not share the former prince's ideals, nor his fondness for lavish spending. Within months, musicians were dismissed, the orchestra dwindled to an *ad hoc* ensemble and Haydn himself grew disillusioned and decided to leave. With a secure bank account and significant retirement investments, Haydn confidently stepped into a world of free-lance artisanship. That's when the offer from J.P Saloman was presented to him. Haydn was eager to accept.

By the fall of 1791, Haydn's 94th symphony was completed and the work was turned over to the music copyists. They were responsible for extracting each instrumental part from the entire musical score. Each voice of the symphony had to be written out for each player of the orchestra. It was exacting work, considering Haydn's symphony included music for the flute, oboe, bassoon, horn, trumpet, timpani, violin, viola, cello and bass. The man selected to lead the copy work was

John Coker, a knowledgeable musician thoroughly trained in his duties. He maintained a reputation of excellence in London and employed a small group of journeymen eager to learn the trade of transcribing music. Coker was a conscientious employer and kept a close eye on the work of each apprentice.

"No room for error," was his motto.

Of Coker's staff, Jonathan Burney was the youngest and least experienced. Even so, Coker admired the quality of Burney's work and thus assigned him the job of copying the first violin part, the most complicated and lengthy of the orchestra. Coker spent a good deal of time looking over young Burney's shoulder. At this point, the young apprentice was well into the third movement, so Coker decided to give his copy work a good once over. He picked up the first two movements. The first movement, the *allegro*, looked excellent. As he turned to the second movement and scanned the opening theme, a horrified look came across Coker's face. Coker shot the young man a wicked look. An outburst occurred.

"Mr. Burney," he shouted, "look at what you have marked at the conclusion of the opening theme! A double *forte*! May I repeat that. You have marked *fortissimo*! I ask you, young man, does it make any sense to indicate a last note to be played full force when the rest of the theme is marked *piano*, a delicate and soft dynamic? Have you taken leave of your senses?"

Burney pleaded, "But Mr. Coker, I only copied what Master Haydn put into his score." With that, he pointed to Haydn's full orchestra score, addressing the very passage Coker had referred to. Coker roughly grabbed the score. There it was, exactly as the boy had said. Indeed, Burney merely had put into the violin part what Haydn had indicated in the orchestra score. The boy had accurately transcribed the notes and their intended dynamic.

Coker mumbled something unintelligible which Burney interpreted to mean that Haydn had possibly written the odd dynamic indication in error. Coker dreaded the next several minutes. Yet he knew what he had to do. He moved across the hallway to the composer's studio. He stood transfixed before the closed door while gaining his confidence. He knocked quietly so as not to disturb the composer. Haydn greeted Coker with a gentle smile.

"What brings you in?" Haydn asked.

"Pardon me, Master, I hate to disturb you, but I fear I have... well rather, one of my assistants....seems to have found an error in your score. I want to correct it with your permission."

"Error? Well, if there is an error, we had best get it corrected now. We wouldn't want all of London to hear something wrong, would we?" Haydn said sportingly.

"The passage in question as at the end of the first phrase of the main theme of the second movement," Coker told him.

"Ah. It's a most pleasant theme, don't you think?" Haydn proposed.

"It certainly is," Coker responded.

Coker took the symphony and opened it to the page that had caused all the commotion. Pointing to the passage, he continued, "But, here in the score, you have marked the final note of the phrase to be played *fortissimo*. I am certain this is in error, considering the remainder of the tune is quiet." Coker said each word with as much tenderness and respect as he could muster.

"Hah!" laughed the composer, "You don't see it, do you?"

"See what?"

"See the joke?"

"I don't understand."

"You don't understand? Then let me enlighten you."

"Please do."

"It's a joke on all of London. Instead of telling you the joke, I want you to imagine you are at the premiere, the room is full of concert-goers, they will have arrived eager to hear the music, yet they will be full from a large dinner. They will have listened to several works that will precede this symphony. They will listen intently for the first movement, then they will begin to relax and fall dreamily into the back recesses of their seats. Imagine all this. Now sing through the passage and imagine what will happen at the moment of the final note of the first phrase."

Haydn paused, then added, "Are you enlightened?"

Coker said he was, but he really wasn't.

He left the room and Haydn began to daydream of the premiere himself. His thoughts took him to the home of Sir Walter Smith and his wife of thirty-seven years, Elizabeth. They were among the many new acquaintances Haydn had met while in London. They were also two of London's wealthiest, and proud of their station.

The Smiths lived in a large, looming domicile not far from the Hanover Square Rooms. The noble residence was dramatic and adorned with a self-important door which was laden with leaded glass. It signaled to anyone who cared to notice that those who lived within its walls were people of great consequence. The house was as cold as winter's chill. Sir Walter Smith was a banker by career and pompous by his nature. As a person of wealth and respectability, he would be expected to make an appearance at tonight's performance of Haydn's new symphony.

Lady Smith had directed the servants to prepare a special dinner for the occasion. She ordered mutton, pork, potatoes, beans and a few choice breads. For dessert, she ordered an extra portion of Yorkshire pudding to be readied.

Sir Walter arrived home half an hour later than usual and both Smiths hastened through their meal. Neither their conversation nor the meal settled well.

Half hour after that, Elizabeth was running several minutes late. She opened the safe, then snorted in haste. "My jewel is missing."

"Which jewel?" demanded Sir Walter.

"The brooch with the large ruby. It is gone!"

"Must you wear that disgusting, flamboyant thing?" Sir Walter demanded. "Why it is so ostentatious that someone might think it gaudy!"

Lady Smith dismissed the thought. After moving a few pieces, she located the prize. In a moment the brooch was affixed to her gown.

They stepped outside greeted by a harsh winter wind that snapped at their faces.

Elizabeth blurted out, "March 23rd. The third day of spring. I would have expected better!"

The Smiths stepped into their waiting carriage and were taken to Hanover Square Rooms, where they would hear Haydn's great symphony.

Haydn was enjoying his reverie. He allowed himself the luxury of continuing the dream.

J.P. Salomon paced the lobby of Hanover Square

Room. Although he was sure he had nothing to be nervous about, a restless tingling in his abdomen reminded him that this was no ordinary night. The idea of bringing the greatest composer in all of Europe to London was his. He was responsible. Tonight, March 23, 1792, would be the night England would remember, or so he hoped. He would ride the coattails of Haydn and achieve a place in history with him.

As the concert hour approached, small groups of friends formed, mostly by gender, in the lobby. Lively conversations ensued.

"They say he is the finest composer in all of Europe," commented one lady, nodding inconspicuously toward Haydn.

"Certainly he is, since the death of Mozart," remarked another.

"It was such a tragedy to lose such a composer. And at the age of 35."

"They say he was buried in a pauper's grave."

In the midst of it all, and at the last possible moment, the Smiths arrived. They found their seats—front row, center, of course, to ensure that they would be seen—and noisily rested in them, first tripping over several ill-placed feet along the way.

As they settled into their places, the first violinist stepped on stage, acknowledged the applause directed to both him and the orchestra, then began the tuning process. All the members of the orchestra had been selected with the greatest of care. Some of the violinists frowned at the sound of the given A, obviously unhappy that the pitch was either too high or too low.

Then the grand moment came. "Papa Haydn," as he had fondly become known, was the last to enter the stage. He was greeted with rousing applause.

"Rather boisterous for London," Sir Walter quipped to his wife.

The applause diminished as the composer assumed his position at the keyboard. He would conduct the concert from there. Haydn's downbeat brought music that filled the room with glorious sounds. Melodies of elegance and charm unfolded. It was carefully written with great spirit and contrived to convey a wealth of emotions. Lady Elizabeth found the music to be sweet as berries, warm as a blanket or fresh as a brook. Every note had a purpose. Nothing was there that needn't be. Every phrase moved toward a goal. Gentle smiles of approval emanated from the musicians and the charm of the music could be seen on the faces of the audience. It was a grand night.

Elizabeth's eyes fell on the composer. He appeared to be pleased by the fine musicians of London. They moved and swayed to the context of each phrase. Even through the most heated of passages, their delight was evident. It was Haydn's night and she was delighted to be part of it. She checked her program and read that the great composer was recognized as the "Father of the Symphony." Rightly so, she thought.

Sir Walter Smith was not sharing his wife's enjoyment of the concert. Fact was, he was quite miserable. Haydn was not to blame. Sir Walter's discomfort began earlier that evening. The banker was not a small man. In fact, he was a man of considerable girth.

When he fell into his seat earlier that evening, he had complained. "I declare. These chairs get smaller each year."

He had to forge his way into its cramped confines. He looked as comfortable as a cat at a bloodhound convention.

As the concert wore on, Sir Walter was feeling the effects of the evening meal. The mutton, pork, potatoes, beans and bread were bad enough. Now he was wishing he had not added that second large portion of Yorkshire pudding. He was cursing himself for such pigishness. As the first movement of Haydn's great symphony was concluding, he found the dinner was growing inside him. He twisted and turned in his seat, but found no relief.

A knock on the door interrupted Haydn's quiet little dream. He was offered a cup of tea and an apology by Mr. Coker who had come to offer his regret for such insolence earlier. Haydn laughed and dismissed the gentlemen. He returned to his reverie.

As the first movement concluded Sir Walter let out just a tiny puff of pungent air. It brought him little relief. However, it did bring on a wicked stare from Lady Elizabeth.

Even Elizabeth was growing tired from the concert. The music of the first movement had given her great satisfaction. She had used every ounce of concentration in order to fully grasp its meaning and beauty. As the slow movement began with its tuneful theme, her head moved in time with the music. Before the tune arrived at the cadence, like Sir Walter, she too was succumbing to the dulling effects of dinner and her eyes were growing heavy. As the tune approached its conclusion, she drifted off into slumber. He though, was already in a deep sleep.

Then it happened. An earthquake could not have had a greater impact. The tune concluded in near silence. That is, until the final note was struck. Haydn raised his arm, which came down swiftly with brute force. The orchestra responded with a mighty sound. *Fortissimo. Double loud.*

The chord roused Lady Elizabeth from her dream. Sir Walter let out a brutal snore that was louder than the orchestra. It snapped the audience as well.

Then laughs could be heard. They began as smiles. Then, snickers of delight followed. Finally, a good guffaw concluded the merriment.

Many in the audience were aghast by such behavior coming from a London crowd of all places. Meanwhile, Haydn was smiling from ear to ear. No one was enjoying the hilarity more than he.

That was all the audience could talk about after the performance. Everyone was so surprised by Haydn's antics.

"Wasn't that a surprise in the second movement?"

The remark was repeated time and time again.

Haydn took great delight in his dream. As he returned to the piano for some more work, he wondered if the concert would really turn out as he had imagined. It did.

Author's note: John Coker, Jonathan Burney, Sir Walter Smith and Lady Elizabeth Smith were fictitious persons.

XI. Incident at the Sistine Chapel in Rome

The carriage ride from Florence, Italy to Rome lasted five days. It was a miserable ride through drenching rain, heavy downpours and mud so deep it touched the hub of the wheels. The carriage was slowed by deep ruts in the passageway that caused several breakdowns. Forward progress was halted on numerous occasions by fallen trees strewn across the road. A these times, it was necessary to stop the carriage, disembark the passengers and remove the debris. Moods grew foul as rain drenched the passengers and their cloaks. Matters were made worse for them when their luggage was soaked. After the fallen trees were removed, the travelers were stuffed back into their tiny riding compartment where everyone was jostled to the point of wracking teeth and crushed bones. Occasionally, the severity of the roadway tossed them onto each others' laps. Then there was the cold. It was the kind of chill that bites at raw bones, makes teeth chatter and shoulders shake. The final injury was the wind that cut to the core. It was a dismal journey.

Wolfgang Amadeus Mozart

The year was 1770. It had begun to rain early in January and simply refused to quit. Now it was the second week of April and still the driving rains continued. It not only drenched them, it dampened their spirits. It put Leopold Mozart and his son in unpleasant moods.

The two were on a musical tour of Italy. While at Florence, they beheld the wonders of its architecture, including the Basilica of the Holy Cross and the Giotto Bell Tower. Though they had been on the road for weeks and were eager to head northward home, the two made an important decision. They resolved to be in Rome for worship services during Holy Week. The determination was actually made by Leopold himself who made all decisions for his family. He ran the family with an iron hand. That's the way he did things. He was, no doubt, a devoted family man, but he had a penchant for guidance that was oftentimes misguided. He dictated nearly every move his son made.

Leopold Mozart was a steadfast member of the Roman Catholic church. With the most holy of weeks just days away, he wanted to visit Rome during the most important week of the church year. Specifically, he and his son would behold the beauties and sanctity of St. Peter's Basilica, home of the Roman Catholic faith. They would cap off their Rome visit by worshiping in the Sistine Chapel.

Leopold was surprised to see his son accept the idea of a visit to Rome. In fact, the boy said he was eager to worship at the Sistine Chapel. Even when Leopold offered his son a choice to return home, the boy said no, he preferred to head south to Rome.

Their conversation was an interesting one.

Leopold suggested, "Wolfgang, we could return to Salzburg without attending Holy Mass at St. Peter's."

Wolfgang responded, "No, Papa, there is no more appropriate place than the Sistine Chapel nor proper time than

Holy Week to worship our Lord. The timing is perfect."

By traveling to Rome, Papa Mozart knew he would give his son Wolfgang the chance to once again hear the music of the Italians. He could learn valuable lessons from such an experience. He told Wolfgang so.

"You could learn much from the Italians while there."

Wolfgang eagerly agreed to make the trip. Papa was surprised by the willingness of his son, particularly because both were so weary from days and days of stagecoach rides. What Papa didn't know was his son had a scheme up his sleeve. Wolfgang was only too happy to make the trip.

"Certainly," the fourteen-year-old Wolfgang said, "let's go."

Leopold wondered why after so many weeks on the road that Wolfgang would be willing to spend an extra five days of traveling, ten if the return ride home was considered. Leopold could not help noticing that his son had been lost in his own world on the journey. He had spent hours looking out the tiny carriage window gazing at the passing landscape. Leopold could even discern a tiny smile that wormed its way across Wolfgang's face. A certain thought troubled Leopold. Was there a scheme forming in his son's head?

There was.

The carriage finally arrived in Rome on Sunday, April 11th around noon. It was Palm Sunday, the beginning of Holy Week. While their travels gave them five days of misery, their spirits were lifted when they arrived in Rome. Clearing skies raised their outlook.

Rome offered Wolfgang the one opportunity to pull off the greatest scheme he could think of. His plan could only be executed in this city. Timing, too, was crucial. He simply had to be in Rome specifically during the week leading to Easter. Of extreme importance was the service on Wednesday the 14th. Attending that service was a must. It was the only way possible for him to execute his plan of intrigue, mystery, and most of all, daring. The carriage ride had provided the time he needed to work out the details of his outrageous idea.

The sun rose brightly on Wednesday the 14th. Morale was running high as father and son arrived at the magnificent confines of St. Peter's Basilica. They made their way to the Sistine Chapel. It was a place of worship amassed with a wealth of paintings that reached across the ceiling from wall to wall. The images were actually frescoes painted directly into the plaster of the ceiling by the great Renaissance master Michelangelo. Immediately, Wolfgang's attention was drawn to the image of two fingers, one of the immortal God approaching that of mortal man. It was a powerful impression that touched the boy.

Although Wolfgang certainly appreciated the exceptionally fine frescoes of Michelangelo, it was not the reason for his determination to be at that particular location on this particular day at this particular service. This day the choir of St. Peter's would perform the *Miserere* of Gregorio Allegri. It was a work that could be sung only two times each year; once on Wednesday of Holy Week and a second time two days later on Good Friday. It had been decreed by the Pope himself.

Gregorio Allegri was a rather obscure composer who lived in the first half of the seventeenth century. His fame rested on one work, his *Miserere*, which took on added fame and intrigue when Pope Urban VIII declared that the work was of such extraordinary beauty and mystery that it could be performed only at the Sistine Chapel. No other cathedral anywhere in Europe would be allowed to experience its mystic beauties firsthand. That would forever belong to the Sistine Chapel. The Pope was so insistent that he ordered that any choir member attempting to remove the music from the Chapel or to write the music down and distribute it to other locations would be excommunicated. It was a punishment that meant banishment from the church. Worse yet, it could end in condemnation to hell itself.

In the opening moments of the Mass, Wolfgang paid scant attention to the service. He was saving his mind for the choir's presentation of the *Miserere*. He was using the time to prepare his enormous brain to accomplish a humanly impossible task. Every neuron in his mind would be engaged. Each would fire, make connections, then drive into his memory the notes he was about to hear.

The glorious music began. It was as Wolfgang had been told. It was music that was mystical, transcendent, glorious, passionate, beautiful and above all else, it was miraculous. It was, in fact, expressly more than all these qualities. The music flowed from its chant-like archaic roots to rich choral harmonies, topped by a glorious high C that transported the young man to an elevating musical experience. For more than nineteen minutes, the music poured forth. Some of it was complex, rich in counterpoint, deep in harmonious content. Other portions were simple, direct, holy without emotion. All were composed to transcend earthly man to heavenly heights.

Mozart thought, "No wonder the Pope has decreed that this music be performed no where else but here, or at any other time than during Holy Week." Mozart listened intently.

On the ride back to his hotel, Wolfgang was exceptionally quiet. He stared at the passing buildings without a sign of emotion. Just a fixed stare. Leopold wondered why.

Upon his arrival at the hotel, Wolfgang seized a stack of blank music manuscript paper. Taking a bottle of ink and a new quill for writing, he moved to a desk. Before taking any more action, the boy stared out of the window, then closed his eyes. He stood motionless for nearly twenty minutes in deep concentration, occasionally nodding his head in a steady rhythm.

Suddenly, he picked up his quill and set to work. As soon as the quill touched the page, notes began to fly on to the paper. Page upon page was filled with notes, hundreds and hundreds of them. He worked feverishly and constantly, stopping only to retrieve another page, fill the ink container or replace a broken quill. The work consumed him. He was lost in it.

While the boy worked, Leopold took notice of his son's characteristics, some of which bordered on peculiar. The boy had a brilliant and extraordinary mind. Of that, there was no doubt. Newspapers were full of descriptions of near superhuman feats produced by his brilliant musical capacities. However, his physical features hardly made him a handsome lad. He was short, which only accentuated his rather large head. His protruding and large blue eyes were set above a large nose. His face was encased in a complexion of yellow, giving him a jaundice look. His countenance was sickly. His cheeks were pockmarked because of an episode of smallpox as a child.

But the boy was gifted with a staggering mind. It was quick...incredibly quick. It was stimulated by Wolfgang's insatiable desire to learn. On this afternoon young Mozart was putting his fantastic mind into high gear. It was beginning to capture Leopold's attention. The boy's work was driving Leopold mad with curiosity. What was the he doing?

"Wolfgang, what are you up to? The curiosity is killing me."

"Oh Papa, it is none of your business."

"What kind of remark is that? Son, my curiosity is turning to anxiety. I demand to know what you are doing."

"Never mind. Papa, this is *my* business."

"Wolfgang, everything you do is my business. I will make it my business to know what you are doing. I have done everything for you...even given up my career for you."

Wolfgang brusquely responded, "And what kind of career is it to be a minor composer in the service of a trivial court in an insignificant city like Salzburg?"

Leopold let it pass, though the comment stung him to the core.

"It may be a minor post, but it does pay the bills, something I trust you will learn for yourself."

Leopold made the remark to remind Wolfgang of his cavalier attitude toward money. Young Mozart simply could not hold on to a penny. Funds slipped through his fingers like water through a sieve. The boy lacked common sense. He was book smart and street stupid. He guessed Wolfgang was using his brain to pull off some nonsensical task. It made him suspicious.

"Wolfgang, you are up to something. I want to know what!" The words were spoken sternly.

"Papa, didn't you always tell me to study the music of the Italians? Over and over, you've told me, 'Learn from the Italians. They have the gift of melody and good humor.' Papa, that is what I am doing. Learning from the Italians."

Wolfgang decided to tease Papa. He held the title page up, just long enough for Leopold's eyes to fall on two words. "Miserere" and "Allegri." Immediately, he understood what Wolfgang was doing.

"You are transcribing the music of the *Miserere*, aren't you?" The realization tore him into a wild rage. "You know that it is forbidden! The Pope has decreed that no one is to copy any page of the music or allow it to be performed elsewhere. To do so could get you excommunicated from the church. Do you understand the severe consequences of what you are doing?"

"Of course I understand that." Then adding with a twinkle in his eye, "The intrigue of this is driving me crazy with excitement."

"Son, may I remind you that excommunication means you are to be removed from the church."

Wolfgang shrugged it off.

"This could mean the condemnation of your soul to the lake of fire."

Wolfgang tried to calm his father down. "Papa, come take a look at this." He opened the first page of the score. With eyes blazing in fury, Leopold began scanning the music. His anger then turned to amazement. There before him was Gregorio Allegri's *Miserere*. Every note perfectly laid out with hardly a correction or erasure to be found.

"Wolfgang, there must be fifteen, even sixteen minutes of music here."

"Papa, it is nineteen minutes, thirty-eight seconds." He made the announcement as if at a royal ball. Pointing to his head, he proudly announced, "It was all up here." Then pointing to the music, "Now it is all there."

He was so excited, he bordered on giddy.

"Son, you will be the death of me."

Then his words dropped in intensity, he grew compassionate and open with the boy. "You are the epitome of musicians. There is no one who is so exceptional. Already at fourteen you write masterful music. I have tried to teach you everything I know, but you far exceed any abilities I might ever hope for myself."

With unabashed confidence and glee, young Wolfgang remarked, "It is an incredible accomplishment, to transcribe a work of such magnitude in just one hearing."

"Wolfgang, your talents exceed any composer in any land. I cannot imagine what the future holds for you."

Wolfgang's life had been a dramatic series of incomparable musical feats. The boy began playing the piano when he was three, picking out tunes at four, composing by his fifth birthday. When he was six, he was playing concerts for the king and queen of France. By the time he was eight, Wolfgang had written his first symphony and an opera by age twelve. Newspapers were filled with articles praising the wonder-child. But this, transcribing the entire *Miserere* in one hearing, went beyond comprehension.

"Are you impressed, Papa?" asked Wolfgang.

"Of course, I am impressed. Are you sure it is correct?"

"Absolutely, it is correct." Then pausing for a moment, "There are a couple of notes I am unsure of. I need to return on Friday to hear it again. Then I can be sure of each note."

Two days later on Good Friday, the two returned to the Sistine Chapel. Again Allegri's mystical score was performed. Wolfgang listened with great intensity. He discovered two notes that needed correction. A mere two notes, out of thousands.

Soon word was out about Mozart's incomparable feat. The news traveled to the Vatican where the pope himself heard of the boy's unbelievable accomplishment. Instead of excommunicating Wolfgang, he bestowed upon him a special award, the Papal Order of the Golden Spur. Mozart was given the rank of knighthood. The boy wore the honor with distinction and called himself "Chevalier Mozart." Mozart liked to think that a knight was made in one day.

XII. Incident at Heilingestadt near Vienna

Ludwig van Beethoven was trapped in a prison. It was not a jail in the usual sense with iron bars and rough-spoken guards. He was caught in a prison of silence. Yet it was not silence devoid of noise. Instead, his world was a cacophony of pounding sounds, garbled clamor and senseless clatter. Had it been total silence, he could have better stood living with such a curse.

Beethoven was not born into silence. Thank goodness for that. The first signs of deafness did not occur until he was a young man maturing into his middle years. He was about twenty-eight when the first sign of any hearing loss occurred. Had it occurred at birth, or even a dozen years earlier than it did, the onset of hearing loss would have profoundly changed his life. Even the whole of music could not have been the same had such an occurrence taken place. So there was some good that came from the fact that it struck him while he was in his twenties.

Ludwig van Beethoven

Beethoven was born a few days before Christmas in Bonn, Germany in 1770. It was a relatively small village of 10,000 people of no particular musical distinction. His father, Johann, was regarded as the town drunk who caused considerable disruption to himself and his family. Though he was a paid bass singer in the church choir, he was also a frequent visitor at the local taverns, where he would remain through much of the night leaving his family at home to care for themselves. In a drunken stupor, he would wobble home in the wee hours, storm into the house and rouse his musically talented son, Ludwig, from his sleep. He demanded that the boy practice the piano. If he refused, the son was beaten severely. A deep hatred developed between the boy and his alcoholic father. The thrashings caused a lifelong rift between the two and helped form aspects of Ludwig's hard-core personality that became his trademark for life. Johann died when Ludwig was seventeen leaving the boy in charge of the family's care. By the time he was twenty, Beethoven was growing restless with his family responsibilities and with the smallness of Bonn.

Though his mother was ill, he headed to Vienna which was becoming the center of the musical world. However, his stay in Vienna was cut short by his mother's death. He returned to Bonn in order to wrap up family affairs. That accomplished, he returned to Vienna and made that city his permanent home for life.

Beethoven was fully equipped with remarkable musical instincts and a tough personality that bode him well as a composer. His native musical skills and the demands his father made that he practice on demand helped to shape a fine musician. In addition to strong piano abilities, Beethoven had a penchant for originality. That was unusual for the times. He had been born into a world dominated by the aristocracy and the church. For any musician to make a reasonable living, the choice was either to serve the secular princely courts or the sacred world of the church. Outside the scope of the opera world, composers were not likely to succeed as free-lance artists.

An undercurrent of independence was sweeping the

world as Beethoven was maturing as a young man. The American and French Revolutions took place before Ludwig reached his twentieth birthday. Though these great events did not impact Vienna directly, the revolutionary spirit of the age, that is, the *zeitgeist*, was beginning to have an effect on the world of art and music. Beethoven became the musical beneficiary of all this.

Beethoven took up permanent residence in Vienna in 1795, a city full of aristocrats who loved music and the arts. However, he was a man of no social distinction. He was a common man, as proven by his name Beethoven. It was a word concocted out of the word 'beet', that is, the vegetable, and the word 'hoven,' meaning garden. The combining of the two created beet-garden, a reference to the fact that the family tradition was linked to farming. It was a profession low on the status structure. Also noteworthy was that he was Ludwig *van* Beethoven, not *von* Beethoven. The use of the "a" rather than an "o" indicates a Dutch connection that evidently went back several generations.

When Beethoven settled in the aristocratic Vienna, he carried little social importance. Though of a lowly peasant background, Beethoven was accepted by those of the aristocracy. They entertained him in their homes. He taught music to their children. They offered him commissions for new works. They were proud to be associated with him. They did these because of his dashing personality and his remarkable piano skills. He was frequently requested to perform private piano recitals in their homes. They were charmed by his playing. It was impressive, dazzling and overwhelming. The recitals usually ended with Beethoven improvising music right on the spot. Such a display of originality became the highlight of the evening.

Beethoven was a complicated man. His behavior could be off putting at times. There was a bit of peasant roughness to him, he was not completely refined. He was also known to be outspoken, saying openly things best left out of conversations with those of higher standing. Some of his brashness was countered by his handsomeness and his charming personality. He also sported bushy and untamed hair of which he was most proud because it showed off his wild spirit.

Although audiences thrilled to Beethoven's piano playing, the Viennese piano of 1795 was hardly adequate for his vibrant spirit. The piano of the day was a light, delicate instrument, hardly like the full-bodied piano developed fifty years later. The Viennese piano did not take too well to Beethoven's piano playing. The piano was too weak for the heavy playing of Beethoven. It succumbed to his brute force. His pounding broke keys, popped strings and bent hammers.

An English piano builder named John Broadwood heard the calling and developed a new piano mechanism that could handle Beethoven's severe beatings. Broadwood's piano was a tougher instrument. That led to an interesting dilemma. When Beethoven was given the newly-improved version of the piano, he challenged it. With it, he wrote music that was more intense than ever. A never-ending cycle began. Beethoven wrote powerful music. A piano was built to take it. That inspired Beethoven to compose music that was yet more powerful. Further mechanical improvements were made to the piano. And so on. Beethoven was more than pushing musical development forward, he was shoving it ahead.

While performing one of his recitals in 1798, a disturbing ringing in his ears occurred. It came, then went away. The ringing began to recur more regularly. Beethoven visited doctor after doctor, all of whom offered a bevy of suggestions, but all of them worthless. He cursed them, calling them quacks. Every remedy failed miserably. The ringing grew so consistent, Beethoven realized with horror that deafness was setting in. It was not a deafness of silence, but one of incessant loud noises and pounding. As he lost his hearing, he was also beginning to lose his way. He withdraw from the public. He grew lonely and came to the disturbing thought that people did not want him. The breakdown of his hearing affected his mind as well as his ears. The onset of deafness began to drive him mad. It led him to think unthinkable thoughts.

Beginning in 1801, at age 31, he spent half a year considering taking his own life. He felt worthless. Who would want a composer who could not hear? What woman would want to claim a husband who could not function normally? These thoughts consumed him until he gave serious thought to ending it all. For six months, he contemplated suicide.

On the other hand, there was a strong-willed side to him that was fostered by the intensity of the hatred between him and his father. It had formed a mighty personality. These two forces, the deafness and his personality, conflicted in an internal war. Finally, he wrote a letter to his brother. In it he told of the great conflict but he also revealed that he had made the decision to continue living.

His letter released the drama and passion of his innermost soul. He poured them into the letter.

"O you men who think or say that I am malevolent, stubborn or misanthropic, how greatly do you wrong me, you do not know the secret causes of my seeming, from childhood my heart and mind were disposed to the gentle feelings of good will, I was even ever eager to accomplish great deeds, but reflect now that for six years I have been a hopeless case, aggravated by senseless physicians, cheated year after year of the hope of improvement, finally compelled to face the prospect of a lasting malady...I was compelled early to isolate myself, to live in loneliness, when I at times tried to forget all this. O how harshly was I repulsed by the doubly sad experience of my bad hearing, and yet it was impossible for me to say to men speak louder, shout, for I am deaf. Ah, how could I possibly admit such an infirmity in the one sense which should have been more perfect in me that in other...What humiliation when one stood beside me and heard a flute in the distance and I heard nothing, or someone heard the shepherd singing and again I heard nothing, such produced all that I felt called upon me to produce, and so I endured this wretched existence. ..O it is not easy, less easy for the artist than for anyone else—Divine One thou lookest into my soul, thou knowest that love of man and desire to do good live therein. O men, when some day you read these words,

reflect that you did me wrong and brother Carl and Johann as soon as I am dead if Dr. Schmid is still alive ask him in my name to describe my malady and attach this document to the history of my illness so that as far as possible at least the world may become reconciled with me after my death. "

Still, the deaf and grief-stricken composer continued.

"To my brothers, recommend virtue to your children, it alone can give happiness, not money, I speak from experience, it was virtue that upheld me in misery, to it next to my art I owe the fact I did not end my life with suicide—Farewell and love each other."

In words that must have cried out to be heard, he finished the testament.

"O Providence—grant me at least but one day of pure joy—it is so long since real joy echoed in my heart. O when—O when, Divine One—shall I find it again in the temple of nature and of men—Never? No—O that would be too hard."

It was not a pleasant decision. It was, however, a decision willed by fate itself. Beethoven had to admit that he had lost control of his own destiny. Fate was responsible for him. He was merely accepting the consequences of destiny. As a result, Beethoven determined he would live not for himself but for the sake of art. Though his life might be lived in a wretched state, his music would inspire him to rise each morning and produce great music, not merely for his own benefit but for the edification of the world. The letter was written in October, 1802, in Heiligenstadt, a part of the city of Vienna. It became known as the Heiligenstadt Testament.

The deafness altered the soul of his music. His earlier works were rooted in the classical spirit of the times. Now he would unleash a new kind of music. It would break free of the confines of the past with its many rules and limited practices. Beethoven's music would be more powerfully expressive, bearing the inner resources of his own soul.

Since he was a boy, Beethoven was fascinated by the French leader Napoleon Bonaparte. They shared similar qualities. Both were short, a few inches over five feet. Each had come from less-than-noteworthy families and hailed from small villages. Both rose to prominence against overwhelming odds, though Bonaparte's rise was in the military and Beethoven's was in the world of music. For years, Beethoven watched the news of Napoleon Bonaparte. He was impressed by the spirit of his victories in the name of liberty. After the French Revolution of 1789, which was followed by Bonaparte's thrilling military victories in the 1790's, Beethoven could see the overthrow of the French monarchy. It could lead to freedom for the common man.

In 1803, though severely handicapped by the developing deafness, Beethoven set out to compose an all-new symphony as a symbol of freedom and the brotherhood of mankind. It would be dedicated to Napoleon Bonaparte. He declared the symphony would embody the spirit of heroism. As a result, the work would be longer, more powerful, more difficult to play and utilize an orchestra of large proportions. When it was completed, it took nearly an hour to perform, at least twice the length of the symphonies of the day.

Days before the premiere of Beethoven's new symphony, Helmut Schniedt heard a knocking on his door. He opened it to find the postman delivering a large package. He unwrapped the box to find the first violin part. He could see by the title it was Beethoven's third symphony. He also read of its dedication to Napoleon Bonaparte, the man who was destined to set the world free.

"Rather surprising dedication," thought Schniedt.

Helmut was being requested to perform for the symphony's premiere. He had heard Beethoven's music before, but had never been asked to play it. He was delighted to be part of the premiere performance. Immediately, he removed his violin from its case and set out to work on the music. The first thing he noticed was the great length of the symphony. It was so long that he was sure there was something was amiss. Possibly the package contained two separate symphonies. Surely not one symphony could be this long. As he begin to practice the music, he was overwhelmed by its difficulty. Finger twisting passages knotted his digits. The fiery tempo and displaced accents constantly upset the normal flow of rhythm. He grew annoyed, uttered a few choice words, then put his instrument down in frustration.

Later that day, he returned to the symphony and determined to see his way through it. He decided the second movement might be easier to play. He was right. He was also impressed with the beauty of its themes. They were warm and wonderful, quite apart from the harshness of some passages from the first movement. Once he had mastered its difficulties, he was inspired to move on to the remaining movements. He began to warm to the symphony.

That is, until he came to the first rehearsal with the entire orchestra. Beethoven was conducting. He was in a foul and difficult mood. It didn't help that he was unable to hear what was going on. The composer was beating time, much too fast for a first rehearsal, and demanding that the music be played with an excessive amount of energy and emotion. Particularly upsetting were the rhythmic requirements of the first movement. The music was written in three beats to the measure, but Beethoven had misplaced so many accents that a feeling of two beats per measure were coming forth. One after another, the players began dropping out. Consternation ruled. This only brought on harsh rebuke from Beethoven. It was a rehearsal of frustration.

The second rehearsal was more productive. Players began to understand the nature of the music and were a bit better prepared for Beethoven's demands. They could also see what the piece was about. Beethoven took the time to explain he sensed the world was changing. The spirit of liberty and the brotherhood of men were unfolding. He was a strong proponent of these changes. His music was meant to express these changes. Though the players were fatigued by its length and the consistent difficulties of the music, they pushed themselves to conquer the symphony and its meaning. It took dedication on everyone's part.

Then it happened. The date was December 2, 1804. Napoleon Bonaparte's victories went to his head. While at the colossal Cathedral of Notre Dame, Napoleon grabbed the crown from Pope Pius VII and declared himself the Emperor. The declaration was followed by a series of wars which became known as the Napoleonic Wars. They devastated all of Europe. More than a million men, women and children were killed. The events rocked the world and sent Beethoven further into depression. In a rage, Beethoven ripped up the dedication to Napoleon and declared it was now a "Heroic Symphony." It still bears the name the *Eroica Symphony*.

The symphony did its share of shocking. Audiences found it difficult to grasp, though they did admire it. Musicians adjusted to its demands causing the players to better themselves as performers. Most of all, it set music free from the restraints of the past. Since its creation, Beethoven has been called "the man who set music free." All composers who lived after him abide in his shadow.

Living in his own prison of silence, with all of its deafening noise, Beethoven had released music from its own prison. Beethoven's prison gave music its freedom. The world of music was changed forever.

Author's note: Helmut Schniedt was a fictitious person.

XIII. Incident at Vienna

It was two hours past noon when Franz Schubert walked toward the café where he would have a late lunch. His pace was a casual one. He was not given to quickness. His stout body preferred a slower gait.

His sluggish speed was quite in contrast to the thoughts whirring through his mind. Thoughts of music and joy were racing through his head. The sun was warm, the air was crisp and in a few moments he would join his friends at their favorite café. Merriment, lively conversation and tasty food were just moments away. Such joys were a worthy reward after a morning stuffed with productive work.

Franz Schubert was a small man. Even at his most upright, he stood hardly an inch over five feet. His diminutive height was symbolic of his statue as a composer. For all his enormous talents, matched by his prodigious work habits, he was hardly known beyond the limits of his own city. He was a man short in stature, and short in reputation as well.

Franz Schubert

He proceeded down several streets, then rounded the corner where the café was located. He was sure his friends were there waiting for him. Schubert knew this because they always waited for him.

His entry was greeted by loud mocking laughter. His musical thoughts had distracted him and he nearly tripped on a chair. The commotion caused everyone's eyes to fall directly on him. The attention disturbed him. He detested it. He had hoped to slip in unnoticed. Still, he knew their outbursts were all in fun.

"Late again!" cried out Johann Mayrhofer, a poet whose words often found their way into the composer's music.

"Hah! I win the bet," laughed Franz von Schober, a friend and admirer of Schubert.

His friends were given to wager on his arrival times, which were as unpredictable as weather. Schubert's mind was void of the concerns of life. He gave little attention to the clock. Time slipped away, much like his money. It too vanished, slipping between his fingers. And without much regret either.

"My friends," young Schubert said, happily taking his place among his beloved group. "I could not pull myself away from my desk. The room was filled with music. I was there, heard it all, and wrote it down as quickly as my pen could move. Melodies kept flowing. My head was spinning with music that came to me as swift as a spinning wheel."

One of his friends, Johann Mayrhofer, another poet, remarked with his index finger flying in the composer's face, "Probably working with one of those wretched librettos again."

Moritz, a fine painter, added, "Franz, you need better texts, finer librettos to match the greatness of your music."

Schubert shook his head. "With so many musical ideas in my mind, I use whatever libretto I can find. For what are words but mere suggestions to hang the music on. I write melodies that enhance the meaning of the poetry, however good or bad it may be."

Franz von Schober asked him, "If you weren't writing an opera, what did you compose today?"

"Several songs," Schubert replied.

That brought around another game of guessing. Mayrhofer wanted to know, "How many songs did you write? I'll wager three." He paused, then remembered that Schubert was a bit later than usual in arriving at the café, so he changed his guess. "No, make that four. I would suppose you completed four songs this day."

Schubert smiled. "Actually, it was six."

That brought Franz Lachner, the conductor of the group, to life. "Six songs! That's unbelievable! Six songs in five hours. That is a song in less than sixty minutes. Franz, you amaze us." Lachner was flabbergasted at the number because he knew Schubert would never compromise on the quality of the songs. They would be of the highest order. Schubert's countless songs were always works of artistry, beauty and originality.

Schubert's commitment to songs brought on a rebuke from the conductor. "Franz, why do you insist on writing songs? Songs are too intimate for our times. They will not do anything for your bank account. Think big, my friend. Think big."

Franz Grillparze, another poet who held a deep admiration for Schubert's works, added, "I agree. Songs will offer you little money. Look at Beethoven who writes large symphonies. His sonatas too are immense and difficult to perform. He thinks big and his music is published all the time. There, my friend, is where the money is. Don't waste your time on songs, an art form that has no future."

Von Schober wanted to know, "Where will these songs be heard?"

Schubert merely shrugged his shoulders. Their concerns were not his.

A brilliant thought struck Mayrhofer. "Why not a series of concerts? I propose we create a series of intimate performances of your music. We can invite a few of our loyal friends to hear your glorious music."

Moritz agreed. "That is an excellent idea. Franz, we are your greatest audience. These, your friends around this table, are the true lovers of your music. But, who are we? We're nothing more than artists living the bohemian lifestyle, barely enough money and just enough food to get by. Yet we live lives of happiness. Carefree too. On the other hand, what if the people of Vienna could hear your exquisite music? They would grow to love and appreciate your mighty gifts. Think of the money that could bring."

The idea was taking shape. Von Schober said, "We insist that the music be only the music of our dear friend, Franz Schubert."

Franz Lachner's next comment sealed the deal. "I have a name for these concerts. They shall be called Schubertiads."

Mayrhofer agreed. "Fantastic thought! Schubertiads! I like it. And we around the table are Schubertians. Let's begin the tradition next week."

Schubert raised the palm of his hand in their directions. Such talk was ludicrous.

His renown as a composer was seriously thwarted by his timidity. He was shy...painfully shy. He never married, hardly played a public concert and was too introverted to seek personal fame. He preferred to do three things: compose, compose and compose.

Because of his shyness, Schubert tried to divert the conversation. "What's to eat?" asked the young composer, as he eyed a couple of half-eaten biscuits on Moritz's plate. He was famished, but had arrived without a penny to his name. He eyed a mutton bone with a good chunk of meat still untouched on Johann's napkin. His mouth watered. He reached for it, but failed to grasp it because his arm was too short. All this to the great delight and ridicule of his friends.

One by one his friends loaded Schubert's plate with their leftovers. This was the common routine. They eat. They leave a little extra. He arrives late. He eats their leftovers. Today was no different than other days. They let out hearty laughs at such outrageous behavior. Even Schubert was having a good time.

"Say, Franz, what did you do for food yesterday when we weren't here?" The question had already been bantered around the table before Schubert's arrival.

Schubert told him, "Herr Schmidt, the owner of the café, traded a meal for a song."

Grillparze was dumbfounded. "You're kidding, right?'

"No," Schubert told him, "I am telling you the absolute truth. I took a napkin, drew the staff lines. Then I picked up my book of Hoffman poems, selected a verse, then walked to the window. I looked across sights of the city for several minutes. As I gazed, an entire song came to me. The melody, the harmonies and the rhythm were all perfectly laid out. I sang the tune through in my head and gave some serious thought to the piano accompaniment. I returned to the table, took the napkin and wrote it all down. Herr Schmidt took the music and in exchange, gave me a hearty lunch."

Moritz shook his head. "You fool! That song could bring you money. Publishers need to learn of your songs."

Von Schober asked, "How many songs have you written?"

Schubert thought for a moment. "Certainly in the hundreds. Most days, I compose two, three or even four songs a day. After awhile, the numbers add up."

Mayrhofer smiled. "Franz, you are an amazing man. All this magnificent music you compose, written right here in the most musical city in the world—Ah! Vienna! Is there another city like it anywhere?— and you cannot secure a buyer for your glorious music?"

Moritz agreed. "Pathetic!"

Mahrhofer continued, "What about opera? I hear there is real money to be made in opera."

The thought of opera had always excited Schubert. Someday, he hoped, a great commission would come his way.

"Sure, opera would be wonderful. I long to compose an opera. In fact, I have already completed several."

Lachner, the resident conductor, joined in, "I've looked over some of your operas. The music is wonderful. The arias would be a joy for any singer. Your melodies demonstrate such a gift." Shaking his head, he spoke more seriously, "It is a shame to waste them on such wretched librettos. Great music and bad texts are a miserable combination."

Von Schober was troubled. "Franz, how can you live, pay the bills, have food to eat if you insist on writing songs or not finding a publisher?"

Schubert laughed. "Money, my friends, who needs money?"

The comment bothered some of his friends. Living the bohemian lifestyle of devil-may-care could not continue forever.

The air was growing a little more tense than Franz wanted. He had come to the café more for the fun than the food. He took a long look around the table. There sat his most dear friends. There was Johann Mayrhofer and Franz Grillparze, both poets; Moritz von Schwind, a painter of growing renown; and Franz Lachner, a conductor who might someday conduct his music. There was also a devoted dilettante, a man of little musical means, but an appreciator and admirer of Schubert's talents. They were his audience. They gave him a reason to be. They offered comfort, friendship and food. At the moment they were getting desperately close to touching a nerve. Seeking fortune or fame was contrary to his deeply imbedded shyness. He decided to clear the air and return to the spirit of gaiety he had come for.

"What do I need of money? I have you, my friends. You always rescue me. What would I do without you?"

Moritz caught the spirit and raised his glass. "Ah, the life of a Bohemian."

Quick outbursts came from each friend.

Schubert began, "No cares."

"Nothing to eat," Moyrhofer said.

"No worries," Schubert responded.

"Nowhere to sleep," added Lachner.

"No concerns," said Schubert.

Then voicing some concern, von Schober added, "No piano for composing?"

The conductor dismissed such a ridiculous thought. "Piano? What piano? The man needs no piano. Have you seen him use a piano? Why the instrument would slow him down."

Schubert certainly did not need a piano to write music that was in his head. The man was a veritable factory of ideas. Yet he was not a machine turning out the same product over and over again. His music was fresh as blooming flowers. His gift for melody was cradled in a series of colorful harmonies that enhanced and underscored each glorious melody.

The laughter continued as the hours passed. One by one his friends moved on their various ways. Darkness came. Still Schubert remained. New customers arrived. Now with a few drinks in him, the composer's inhibitions subsided and he moved to their tables. Dancing took the place of eating. The café was becoming a din of noise and uproarious behavior. He was in the midst of it all, dancing, partying until he finally wearied. Soon all were gone. Left alone, he wallowed in his thoughts. He ended the day by wobbling home, his stout little body showing the impact of too much drink and too little food.

He arrived at the flat he shared with Moyrhofer, Grillparse, Moritz and Lachner. Schubert, exhibiting considerable dizziness from the evening's activities, asked himself, "I wonder which bed will be mine tonight."

Then he fell onto the couch and into a deep sleep.

Such a day was typical for him. His first twenty-three years were joyous ones creating upbeat, buoyant music that bubbled like an effervescent fountain. He spent his days carefree with a happy-go-lucky attitude toward life itself.

Suddenly his life changed. Tragedy struck in the form of illness. A sense of his early death began to pervade his mind. It affected his music. It grew darker, more restless. In some cases, it exuded a sense of hollowness. Schubert continued to turn out music, but its content revealed a man expressing more ominous and shadowy thoughts.

When Schubert was thirty years old, a great and tragic event hit Vienna. It occurred on March 26, 1827. Word spread rapidly, like a wildfire in a gale. Ludwig van Beethoven was dead! Although the news was not a surprise, for the man had often complained of one malady after another, its impact was profound.

Schubert learned of the tragic news on his way to the café. The newspapers were filled with final tributes of praise for Beethoven, the colossal figure who had given a wealth of magnificent music to the city. Concerns for the future of music were also expressed in the papers. Who could take his place? Who could follow in the footsteps of a giant?

A heavy gloom hung over the table that morning.

"Franz, certainly you've heard the news?" said Mortiz, half as a question and half as a statement.

Schubert nodded. He did not feel like talking. The death of Beethoven was serious enough, but Schubert himself was in a depression deeper than usual today. The passing of Beethoven had prompted thoughts of Schubert's own deepening illness. Thoughts of his own demise were looming. They were becoming serious. The fact was, he welcomed thoughts of his own passing. Death could end all his troubles. Was it really all that bad?

The sight of his friends lifted his spirits somewhat, but did not dampen his morbid thoughts entirely.

Lander had attended Mass earlier that day. "I have heard that officials of the church are looking for you Franz. I believe you will be asked to be a carry a torch for the funeral procession of Beethoven."

Schubert reacted with a quick raise of the eyebrow. "That comes as a surprise. I would be honored to serve in such a humble capacity." To carry a torch for the great Beethoven was not insignificant. Schubert was moved. He left his friends, preferring not to converse. He made his way to the church to seek the details. A priest took Schubert in.

"Yes, Herr Schubert, Beethoven himself has requested that you carry a torch at his funeral. It was in his will and it is quite an honor."

"The request surprises me, Father," said the shy composer. "There was a time I met the great Beethoven at a restaurant. I was in much fear of the man. Although I was not sure he knew me or my music, he said he admired my music. I was astonished to hear him say it."

Just a year later, Schubert, himself, was placed into the earth, his life taken from him by a complication of diseases. Unlike Beethoven's funeral, Schubert's memorial service drew only limited interest, attracting just a few friends.

Vienna had begun to take notice of Schubert after Beethoven's death. One concert given exclusively to his music was open to the public in his final year. It caused a minor stir and more importantly received good reviews. However, the recognition came too late and was of too little value to raise the awareness of his musical genius. His dear friends were overwrought with grief. They could only think of what might have been.

And what was left at his death? His works formed a staggering list of more than eight-hundred compositions, composed by a man who lived just thirty-one years. He left behind nine symphonies, one was unfinished. Oddly, it became his most famous. He left drawers filled with large quantities of string quartets and piano pieces. Many of these never were given a playing in his lifetime. Schubert wrote them, put them away, then forgot them. They were scattered all over Vienna.

Most remarkable of all were his songs. Over six hundred of them. They comprised some of the most beautiful and poetic melodies ever written. They beg the question, what might have been?

XIV. Incident off the Coast of Scotland

Felix lived life at a hectic piece, flying from one frantic activity to another. Fortunate for him, he was a highly capable person who could do practically anything, and do it exceedingly well. Because of his great intellect, he learned things with ease. Then, too, he was diligent. He studied incessantly on a variety of subjects and practiced his musical skills diligently. He also was a man likely to over-commit himself, accepting one too many activities or appointments. Besides all those marvelous qualities, he was also a compliant person, even as a child. He respected authority and fervently worshipped tradition. The man was well loved and highly respected.

Felix Mendelssohn

Felix was also a nervous person. Anxiety was his constant companion. As one intent on being the best, he never accepted second place. For all the remarkable qualities he possessed, he insisted on developing each one of them to its fullest potential. It often resulted in physical and mental exhaustion. Sometimes, it evidenced itself in illness and on an occasion or two, came close to bringing on nervous breakdowns. He was a man focused on being the best and driven to push himself to untold limits. Such personal characteristics caused him great apprehension and angst.

He possessed interests in all sorts of subjects. Although he could have chosen a number of careers: law, banking, or commerce, he chose music as his true love. His musical talents were remarkable. He demonstrated formidable piano skills, dynamic abilities as a conductor, and as a composer, he surpassed nearly everyone else of his day. Had he decided on a career as a violinist, he would have been the finest in all of Germany, or even Europe for that matter. It seems there was nothing he could not do.

Felix Mendelssohn was born in 1809 in Hamburg, Germany, directly in the middle of one of the most cultured societies in Europe. He was raised in a world of music during the early nineteenth century when Germany was at the top of the musical world. Beethoven and his colossal reputation reigned supreme. The music of Mozart, Haydn, Bach and Handel were readily available for study and practice. These offered a boy whose family was steeped in the arts, an ideal background for development.

He was born to Abraham and Leah Mendelssohn, reasonably well-to-do and cultured parents who were fully intent on giving their children every advantage. They insisted that their two children, Felix and Fanny, be extremely diligent about their studies. Both children were required to up by 5 A.M. to begin studies of history, the sciences, literature, painting and of course, music.

The endless days of study paid off handsomely for both

Felix and Fanny. By the time she was thirteen, Fanny had memorized the entire set of Bach preludes and fugues from the *Well-Tempered Clavier*, a feat only a few concert pianists of the twentieth century would likely attempt. As for the boy, Felix knew Beethoven symphonies by heart and could play many of them at the piano.

Abraham Mendelssohn also offered his son something amazing for any budding composer: a whole orchestra for which he could practice composing and conducting. It paid handsome dividends.

As a youth Felix produced compositions of amazing maturity. Some of the works written in his teens displayed genius qualities. In fact, one of his most famous works, the *Midsummer Night's Dream,* written when he was seventeen, displayed amazing wisdom and experience. In a short time it achieved the stature of a work worthy of international fame. It was practically a perfect work.

Practically a perfect work. Perfection suggests every note was exactly in place, as it indeed was. Each harmony and twist of melody was carefully calculated. The orchestra remained precisely in balance, allowing each note of each phrase to be heard in its exactitude. And, above all else, the emotions were held in balance so as not to overwhelm the perfection of each note. The flavor of the music was light as a feather. It was the ideal textbook piece. The heart and the mind were in a model state of equilibrium in *Midsummer Night's Dream.*

By the time he was twenty, he began an extensive tour that lasted three years. He covered every important center of Western Europe including England. He performed piano concerts, conducted orchestras and kept a busy composing schedule as well. He met hundreds and hundreds of people who adored him. He wrote long, detailed letters to these acquaintances. In addition, he made penciled drawings and sketches of the faces of those he met; they were perfect sketches, pure representations, though hardly perceptive ones that revealed aspects of their personalities. He refrained from emotional portrayals. He drew only what he saw.

On a crisp day in the summer of 1829 Mendelssohn took leave of his overbearing concert activities for a brief holiday. While on vacation visiting Scotland, a friend, Sir Walter Scott, offered him an outing on a row boat. Scott wanted to show Mendelssohn one of the natural glories of the North Sea. It was Fingal's Cave. Together they rowed out some distance from the rocky shoreline where they found the ideal location to eye one of nature's most fascinating sights: Fingal's Cave, known to some as the Hebrides. It was a sea cave carved out by the restless waves of one of the world's roughest oceans. The mysteries and intrigue of the caverns immediately caught the attention and imagination of the composer. The agitation of the waters, the lava formations that formed the geological shapes at the entry suggested to him images that could be interpreted musically. In his mind, he pictured the interior of the cave, a place of haunting beauty, of restless foreboding and of deep intrigue.

Immediately an orchestral work began to take shape in his mind. Inspiration descended on him. Right on the spot, Mendelssohn jotted down the opening theme. He dashed off a letter home. In it, he wrote, "In order for you to understand how extraordinarily the Hebrides affected me, the following came to my mind there." Within the letter he attached an addendum which contained the first twenty measures of music that would become the opening of a descriptive concert overture.

After that momentary inspiration, Mendelssohn put *Fingal's Cave Overture* aside. The project lay dormant for some time. He had other appointments and concerts to fulfill, as he resumed his fast-paced travel routine. Mendelssohn headed south to Italy for more performances. After an extended tour, he turned his attention to the imaginations of Fingal's Cave and set out to complete work on the piece. He envisioned a concert overture, a descriptive piece for the orchestra of moderate length...some ten or so minutes.

It was quite unusual for Felix to compose a concert overture. Such concert overtures were a new thing in 1830. He was not given to employing such nontraditional fancies, he was a man steeped in the past. Why, he had often told his sister Fanny, "Do not commend what is new until it has made some progress in the world and acquired a name, for until then it is a mere matter of taste." The comment was evidence that his tendencies were to move cautiously, proof enough that he was a traditionalist at heart. The world of music in the opening quarter of the nineteenth century was undergoing new innovations, geared to the emotions. It displayed them as never before. With its emphasis on personal feelings, it was referred to as romantic music. Not romance in the sense of love, but because of the exposure of raw and personal passions.

While most younger composers of Germany were attracted to the aims of romanticism, Mendelssohn remained somewhat out of step with his contemporaries. He avoided throwing his emotions too deeply into his music. To do so, he felt would negatively impact the structure of his music. Music that stemmed more from the heart than the head left him uncomfortable. To Mendelssohn's thinking, these romantics ignored balance of structure and form. They were sacrificed to express the passions of the individual. On the other hand, he preferred the objectivity of Mozart, a man dead for nearly forty years. The past was the model for his music. That is how Mendelssohn thought.

Even with such a traditional outlook, he set out to create a descriptive piece about the sea. To use music to describe nonmusical events was quite out of the ordinary in composition of the past. Beginning around 1820, the forward-looking composer Carl Maria von Weber, impressively created a feeling of the forest in his opera *Der Freischutz*. Though music is quite unable to actually describe anything, it does have the power to portray the mystery, emotions evoked and on occasion, the rhythm of places. Yet Mendelssohn's backward leanings would normally have prevented him from trying to describe a sea cave. Something unique and powerful about Fingal's Cave must have impacted him.

Mendelssohn employed a new musical technique known as tone-painting in *Fingal's Cave Overture*. Tone-painting involves depicting images or suggesting nonmusical elements in the music. Within *Fingal's Cave Overture*, he captured the essence of restless waves. The undulations of the sea and the interplay between it and the wind were brilliantly woven together. The opening theme, given to the rich sounds of the cello, was among the finest melodies he ever wrote. The work descended into the cavernous spaces conjuring up images of an unsettling nature. The listener can almost envision the strange colors and the vastness of its interior. It proved that when he chose to employ techniques of the romantics, he could do so with the best.

Mendelssohn's extensive travels and busy routine finally caught up with him. In 1837, at the still-young age of thirty-eight, his body just could not take it anymore. Endless deadlines, countless days of stagecoach rides, night after night of staying in hotels, followed by meeting people wore him out physically. Added to these were numerous piano recitals, conducting appearances and commissions for new compositions. It was too much. They did him in. Still, he pushed himself on. His letters home began to hint at his exhaustion. His family was worried about him. From England he wrote, "If I stay one more week in London, it will kill me."

He immediately departed for his German homeland. Still, his nervous nature took over and once again he found himself overcommitted.

While working himself to near exhaustion on yet another tour, a letter arrived. It told of sister Fanny's stroke, which took place in May, 1847. In a matter of days, she slipped away. The impact of the news made him realize he had to slow down. He moved to Switzerland, where his days there were occupied with painting and some limited composing, which helped calm him.

Then he, too, was stricken with a stroke, followed by a second. On November 4, 1847, at just thirty-eight, he succumbed to a life lived like a candle burning at both ends.

Unlike his perfectly balanced compositions, Mendelssohn's life was lived like a runaway train.

XV. Incident at Paris

Franz Liszt checked the image in the mirror. He was impressed by his own reflection. He was handsome, as good looking as a prince. Even he could admit that. His perfectly shaped narrow face and clear complexion were immediate attention getters. His good looks had already served him well. The mirror only proved what most ladies already knew. He was dramatically attractive.

Liszt had been gifted with flowing facial features that were matched by a lean and trimmed torso. From his forehead to his toes, he was a fine specimen of fluidity. Most striking was his flamboyant hair. It flowed to his long cheeks. From there, the eye was carried on through a graceful neckline and shoulders, which ran on to his lean limbs. From head to toe he was handsome. Not just handsome, he was dashing. Striking too. Only his deep-set eyes and furrowing brows gave a hint there that might be another side to him. His deep-browed eyes suggested something of a devilish personality. In a few minutes, his audience would see that side too. Yes, he knew, there was no doubting that his coming out on stage would foster images of one who was both handsome and devilish. He also knew his looks would foster dramatic displays of emotions, particularly from the women.

Franz Liszt

Taking his eyes off the looking glass, he checked his fingers. Like the rest of him, they were long. They were lean. They were dexterous. He placed them on the dresser and tested them. They moved with grace, as fluid as water. They were facile with an agility that was legendary. His hands and fingers, like his reckless lifestyle, were known throughout all of Europe. Like every other audience he had bedazzled, Liszt knew that in a few minutes, this audience would be transformed from mere concert-goers to star-struck fanatics. His fingers were highly trained to do the impossible. Tonight he would prove it to the people of Paris, his adopted city.

Returning to the mirror, he straightened himself, raised his head, then flicked his upper body in a dramatic gesture. The force threw his hair in triumph.

"Ah, yes, the hair," he said to his reflection in the mirror. "That will dazzle the ladies." And he was right.

The dramatic gesture had thrown his hair into a tousle, yet it was all done in a carefully calculated manner. His locks were long; long enough to touch his shoulders. He had brushed his mane to give the appearance, not of perfection, but of wildness. That way, his effect on them would prove to be more dramatic. As he gave another flick of his head, his hair lifted off his shoulders and it flew across his face. It fell over his eyes.

"Perfect," he said, "that will give them the impression I cannot even see the keys. Yet I will play on, faster, and with more drama. That will amaze the ladies even more."

That is what he wanted. That is what he knew they wanted. Liszt was not a man to disappoint them and neither was he about to let himself down. He desperately wanted their attention.

Now, one final look in the mirror. He tugged at his coat and tails which were richly adorned with jewelry suspended with chains. Such adornments complemented and completed his outfit. In a few moments he would step onto the stage and the audience of Paris would be struck by his princely appearance. Even though he wasn't a prince, his great abilities made him believe he was worthy to be called a prince. That's the way he thought. The public image he had created for himself was certain to generate great cries and gasps of delight. Liszt also knew after such outbursts greeted him, a transformation would take place. He would convert himself from prince to virtuoso. It was going to be a grand night. He knew it.

Meanwhile, ladies were gathering in the lobby. The excitement was driving them mad. Their exchanges bordered on the ridiculous.

Lady Marie Peugot, who always had a fondness for gossip and empty discourse, broke the ice among her friends. "I heard Liszt in Brussels. I swear he took the breath away from every lady in the concert."

"I can confirm that," said Marianna Lamond. "The papers there reported several ladies fainted during the performance."

Francois Dumas wasn't so sure. She uttered, "I find that difficult to believe. How could a pianist, even a virtuoso performer like Liszt, induce one to fainting? I say it is all rumor."

Overhearing their conversation, Clara Rosenthal visiting from Munich, imposed herself into the conversation. "Ladies, I can confirm that when Franz Liszt came to Munich, ladies were overcome. Indeed, they did faint." Then adding in a whisper to the dumbfounded group, "There was a report that one woman was so overwhelmed by Liszt and his performance, a doctor was called and she was rushed to the hospital."

Not to be outdone, Henrietta Margot hit them with the surprise of the night. She opened the locket she wore with delight. Out popped a hideous and dark brown object not much bigger than a large coin.

"Whatever is it?" demanded Lady Peugot, reeling back in revulsion.

"It's a cigar butt. Liszt, himself, smoked the cigar. I retrieved it, then promised I would wear it near my heart until I die. It is a promise I will never fail to keep."

"That seems a bit outrageous to me," remarked Marianna.

"Outrageous? Maybe. Yet, it is my treasure," Henrietta told them. She even thought she saw an eye of envy in one of the ladies.

That scene was replicated in other small circles over and over that evening.

The men were not so overwhelmed. They could agree that Liszt had a distinguished reputation as a virtuoso pianist. They had other concerns, and these were about his character.

"The man is a charlatan, a true con artist." The remark was made by Francis Belmond, a conductor who had heard Liszt perform on numerous occasions. "His concerts are nothing more than show pieces that are meant to dazzle and befuddle."

"The man is a grandstander," added Alfred Reisner, "something I cannot stand in a man."

"That may be true," insisted Frederic Mannheim, "but I have come to hear the man play the piano. From all the news I have heard, he outplays every musician in the land."

Georges Fortenet relayed an experience of many years earlier. "I heard him when he was hardly more than a boy. I can confirm his remarkable abilities as a pianist. Even more amazing, I believe he was thirteen at the time. He had the prodigious talents of Mozart. He was astonishing even as an adolescent."

"What disturbs me most," Charles Fennet said, shaking his head in disgust, "is his self-centeredness. He takes great liberties of tempo. His interpretations go beyond the nature of good music making. He believes himself better than the master composers of the past. I find such arrogance sickening."

Both camps were correct. Each group revealed truths about the man. As the ladies had found, he was handsome, debonair, dashing and extremely eye-catching. On the other hand, men viewed him correctly as a man set on himself, self-serving, a charlatan. Their images stemmed from their point of view.

Liszt was also a man ahead of his time. He saw what other musicians either chose not to see or decided not to follow. The public loved to be entertained as much as they loved great music. He was happy to oblige their desires for entertainment.

Liszt was a celebrity of his day. However, he was not the only superstar. There was a violinist, Nicolo Paganini, who also was a virtuoso, a ladies man and a musical hero. When Liszt was twenty years old, he first heard the Italian violinist. Liszt watched Paganini with rapt attention, which nearly bordered on envy. Liszt saw Paganini's ability to overwhelm his audiences. He played his violin with a virtuoso and flamboyant style that was matched by a mad, devilish behavior. He broke strings, but continued on. He performed unheard-of feats on the violin. He played faster, louder, with more passion than any player before him. Legend has it that Paganini may have been the greatest violinist in all of history. He also was Liszt's inspiration.

Paganini drove Liszt mad with excitement.

"Why," he told himself, "could I not do with the piano as Paganini has done with the violin?"

Such a goal drove him to practicing four, five, even six hours a day. His days were filled with practicing double octave passages, rapid scales, trills, embellishments; they were drilled repeatedly over and over again for two years. Gifted with large hands and nimble fingers, even as a boy, his teachers could not contain him. They passed him on to teachers of greater repute than themselves. Nothing stopped him. Such natural gifts, when trained to perfection, then complemented with a fiendish desire for fame, drove Liszt to untold heights of self-importance. He emerged from his self-driven rehearsals two years later, aged twenty-two, ready to thrill audiences throughout Europe.

Tonight, as the year 1850 approached, the Parisian audience would be dazzled by a new stunt from Liszt. He was prepared to go it alone. He would perform the entire concert without assistance from another artist. This was his concert, his alone, and he had dubbed the performance a 'recital.' The word "recital" was new to the public. It was, in fact, a word he had invented himself. He used the word to carry the message that he would recite (therefore giving life to) the notes in a program dedicated to him as a soloist. He was a man who needed no one else. He had no intention of sharing the stage, or especially the limelight, with another musician. Why lower himself? He would go beyond being just a pianist, Liszt intended to become their hero-musician.

As the hour of the recital approached, Liszt made his final preparations. He ran his fingers through his hair to give himself a just-slightly look of disarray. It was a coiffure to amplify his wildness. His last glance at the looking glass drew a nod of approval. He was ready.

The appointed hour arrived. The audience was seated. As the lights dimmed, Liszt, with heart pounding and fingers wiggling anxiously, moved to the edge of the stage. He caught a glimpse of the room. It was full. As the last wax-lamp was lowered to the properly dimmed level, silence fell on the hall. All motions ceased. Every movement was suspended. Even the great clock appeared to stop.

The hall was a wild mixture of scents that fused together odors of melting wax, an array of perfumes and perspiring people. In a moment these smells would go unnoticed in the dazzling display that was about to unfold.

After waiting till the last dramatic moment, Liszt took an upright pose, then walked with effortless grace across the stage. He was adorned as a highly decorated officer bedecked in jewels and chains. His first step on stage ignited his audience. With every succeeding step their applause grew more thunderous. As it reached riotous proportions, he bowed deeply taking in every detail of the night. He even caught the eyes of several beautiful ladies. He relished this. His performance tonight would launch him beyond the stage of a pianist. Tonight he would become a hero. More than that, he would become a god. Of this, he had no doubt.

After stretching the applause to its limits, he turned and moved to the piano with the grace of a ballet dancer. Each movement had been carefully thought out and crafted. Slowly he removed his gloves. With near reckless abandon, he tossed them toward the first row. Several ladies moved forward to capture these treasures, then halted against their better judgment. He caught the anxious delight in their eyes.

He carried nothing with him but his magical fingers. Not a script of music was to be found. Every note was memorized. Each passage committed to his heart. He would play thousands of notes and each one plucked from the recesses of his mind. No one else, not another pianist in all of Europe, would attempt such a brash undertaking. It was calculated to bring the house down.

Liszt took his seat at the immense piano before him. It was a monstrosity stretching nine feet across the stage. Within the course of the evening, it would be pushed to its furthest limits. Its eighty-eight keys would be pounded, its hammers pulverized, its strings stretched and tested to their fullest potential. Under his command, they would be beaten into submission. The pounding would be relentless. It would come full force. It would be constant, riveting and mesmeric. From its innermost workings to its passive and massive lid, Liszt would push the machinery of the instrument and the whole of pianism to never-heard-of limits.

The audience sat in hushed silence. Liszt was in absolute control—and he had not even played a note. He took a deep breath taking in the scents of the night as well as the spirit of anticipation that emanated from every music lover.

The moment of truth was now at hand. With a dramatic uplift of his hands, his arms fell upon a ferocious chord that echoed off every surface. It punctuated every ear drum in the hall. From there Liszt rattled off impressive passages of double octaves, scales that were played at breakneck speed and trills that were executed with the power and drama of a military band. Even though the audience had anticipated this, it sat in sheer amazement at his superhuman skills. Each bravura passage was delivered with the drama of a tiger in full chase.

Although Liszt possessed immense abilities as a pianist, he was guided by a cavalier attitude toward the aims of each composer.

He had been heard to say, "What does it matter that I play exactly what each composer has written? It is far more impressive to perform the music as I see it."

What he had failed to admit is that he had compromised the intentions of the composer. He had dared to rewrite the Masters. Beethoven, Mozart, Haydn, Bach and Handel were subjugated to Liszt's whims. To their carefully crafted masterpieces, he freely added notes. He did this to electrify the listener. Their masterpieces were subjected to octaves where single notes had been written. This, he did, not to edify, but to stupefy.

None of this mattered to Liszt. He was thinking beyond the confines of a piano. He was transforming the music. The piano was becoming a whole musical ensemble. What had been composed for the piano, he renovated into pieces for the orchestra. Each key became an instrument. Its eighty-eight keys were now eighty-eight players. Liszt released the sounds of horns, flutes, oboes, trumpets, cellos, violins and the timpani. All created from the keys of the piano. That was because he was a god.

Tonight was his and he was theirs. That is all that really mattered.

Author's note: All the men and women in the lobby were fictitious including, Marie Peugot, Mariana Lamond, Francois Dumas, Clara Rosenthal, Henrietta Margot, Francis Belmond, Alfred Reisner, Frederic Mannheim, Georges Fortenet and Charles Fennet. (The story of a women [told here to be Henrietta Margot] wearing a bracelet filled with Liszt's cigar butt is a true one.)

XVI. Incident at Prague

The city of Prague sits upon the banks of the River Moldau in central Bohemia. Not only has it been the political, cultural and economic center of Bohemia for over 1000 years, Prague is also known to be one of the most beautiful cities in all of Europe. Over the centuries, its natural beauty has been enhanced by spectacular architecture creating a city with such nicknames as "the mother of cities," "city of a hundred spires," and also the enticing title, "the golden city." By all standards, Prague is a special city.

Bedrich Smetana

Located deep within the heart of Europe, Prague has remained among the most visited cities on the European continent. That has been true for a thousand years. Unfortunately, it is also a city that has been visited by political turmoil. For centuries, its central location has put it directly in the crosshairs of conflicting empires and dominions at war with each other.

In the year 1848, Prague was becoming a hotbed of political agitation. The Kingdom of Bohemia was governed by outside forces. For the previous thirty-three years, beginning with the Congress of Vienna of 1815, Austrian forces were in control of Bohemian lands. The Austrians had purged many of the liberties of the Bohemians. It caused frictions. Along with other ethnic nationalities, including Poles, Serbs, Romanians and Hungarians, the people of Prague longed for greater personal and political freedom.

Bohemian folks were often heard to complain, "Why should foreigners, those Austrians, run our lands? What do they really know of us?" In 1848, resentment was growing from discontent to outright rebellion.

At the time, Prague was a multi-faceted city. It was naturally beautiful. As a community, it was rich in its cultural history. Within its city limits, there could be found a wealth of architecture, museums, galleries and musical ensembles. Yet by 1848, beyond a short list of names including Jan Dussek, Vaclav Tomasek, and Jan Vorisek, few Bohemian composers achieved significant and international fame. Though these composers were talented, none achieved enough acclaim within their country to become a rallying point for a national school of composition to form.

That is, until Bedrich Smetana, entered the scene.

Smetana's story begins in 1824, when he was born in the city of Litomyslf, Bohemia where his father ran a brewery. From an early age, he displayed phenomenal talents as a musician. At the tender age of five, he was a strong enough violinist to perform in an amateur string quartet, itself, no small accomplishment. Not limited to the violin, young Bedrich gave his first public piano performance at age six. When he was eight, he proudly proclaimed, "I want to be a composer in the tradition of Mozart." It brought a severe reprimand from his father who advised his son to refrain from such nonsense as to consider a career in music. Still, young Bedrich pushed forward with his musical studies best he could, until he was nineteen. Only then was he able to begin serious academic studies of music.

Though it may have lacked for homegrown composers, Prague was very much alive with a variety of musical offerings. The city was enticement enough for Smetana to make it his permanent home.

Though Prague was a place of immense beauty and musical activity in 1848, it was becoming a political hotbed. Civil discourse was coming close to boiling into civil disobedience. Resentment against the Austrians and Hapsburgs was running high among the citizens of Prague, especially the younger generation, of which Smetana was a prime example.

In the cafés, over a drink or two, Smetana could be found caught up in discussions with his fellow musicians, complaining. "Why can't we Bohemians have our own kind of music…something that stems from the spirit of our own land? Do the Germans always have the power to control our music?"

"What do you propose?" asked Jan Clovicek, a promising pianist who shared some of Smetana's concerns, though not to the same degree.

Smetana expressed his viewpoint, "At this point in time, I'm really not sure what I mean. But one thing I do know, we must find our musical identity as a nation, then capture it and create a music that expresses the zeal and flavor of our own land."

"You mention the Germans. What is the aggravation there? They produce fine composers of excellent music."

"I agree they create excellent music. But it is *their* music, expressing *their* ideals, *their* traditions, *their* way of thinking. As a Bohemian first, and a musician second, I insist we must find a music that is our own."

"Why not consider using the music of the French composers as a model for a new kind of music."

"The French? Certainly you jest!"

"What's the problem with French music?"

"Everything about French music has been locked up in the courts of all the Kings whose names are Louis. I can't even remember what number the present King Louis is!"

"Actually, there is not even a Louis on the throne today. Napoleon III is the monarch."

"Still, the royalty in France holds all the money, which means the emperor's favorites get picked to compose music that suits the taste of the court."

"What do you think of the Italians?"

"First of all, the Italians do produce a fresh kind of music. I'll hand them that. They have demonstrated great originality in their music. I find Italian music to be joyous and richly melodic. However, Italy is such a jumble of city-states, no *single* kind of music has emerged. Not a music that reflects the spirit of the people who belong to a real nation. However, I think if Italians settled on one national spirit of music, it could be quite remarkable."

"Spain?"

"Ah, yes, Spain. There is a country with a unique kind of music. With all the Moorish invasions, Spain is home to a real cross-section of cultures, both Eastern and Western. Because of that, Spanish music is quite different than the learned music of the rest of Europe. The music is highly colorful, dramatic and emotional, all of them fine qualities. However, the dramatic flair of Spanish music overwhelms other important elements of music, such as harmonic innovation and complex counterpoint. As a result, for me, Spanish music becomes all too much of the same stuff."

"What about England?"

"England? England has hardly produced more than a couple of worthy native composers. It took composers like Handel and Haydn to offer Londoners some great musical experiences and both of them were Germans."

"All right, if we agree that we Bohemians should form our own musical voice, where would we start?"

"Why not with folk dances? Possibly it could be folk legends. Think of the fantastic stories the people of the villages know and tell. Especially those tales around a fire at night in the village square. What great music might come out of that!"

"Bedrich, your Bohemian music ideas will just have to wait until we rid ourselves of those cursed Austrians. With all the restrictions on our personal freedoms instituted by those foul Austrians, Bohemians simply worry about living from day to day. I am afraid, music will have to wait its turn."

Smetana raised his voice, "I, for one, am not about to wait one more day!"

Bedrich's friend spoke not only for himself, he also reflected the sentiments of others in Prague as well. They too could not understand the need for a national kind of music. More times than not, Smetana's nationalistic ideals fell on deaf ears. Sometimes his fellow countrymen were demonstrably hostile toward him. Yet, he was a stubborn man committed to his own ideals. Though misunderstood, he pressed forward with developing a kind of music built directly from the great Bohemian spirit.

He left the café for an underground meeting with other political malcontents. It was a meeting of Bohemian patriots and he counted himself as one of them. The meeting that night was mostly an orderly one, with the airing of grievances about foreign military forces in their city and the suppression of personal liberties. Some talk coming from the hardliners opened up discussions of open rebellion and war in the streets. Such discussions concerned him. Smetana sought to move forward with more caution. Usually, he kept his political views at such meetings close to his heart. However, on an occasion or two, he spoke out briefly at these assemblies.

Following a few meetings, the patriots grew more restless and talk turned to action. An open revolution broke out. It was severely and quickly quashed. In the months that followed, Smetana remained one of the patriots closely watched by the government. Over the next half dozen years, he remained under suspicion.

While still in Prague, his political leanings seriously jeopardized the possibility of advancing his career as a composer. In 1856, he headed to Sweden where he assumed the position as conductor of the Gothenburg Orchestra. Conducting the orchestra taught him a great deal about composing for such an organization. He developed a deep sense of the broad array of timbres of the orchestra. He learned the rich musical literature of composers from various countries. The conducting further strengthened his musical ear, which already was keen and acute.

In 1862, he returned to Prague. Word had reached him that tension in the air was clearing and the city was transforming itself back to its old ways. The Austrian political hold was beginning to weaken. Best of all, a new musical concert house, the Provisional Theater, had just opened. It provided a feeling of resurgence in the citizens and a new opportunity for Smetana.

His dream of a national Bohemian school had never faded, even in the years spent in Sweden. In fact, his vision was enhanced as he took in the sights of the sea, the magnificence of the mountains and the darkness of the incessantly long winters. All these suggested that geography itself might shape the people and their art. His ideas for a national form of Bohemian music only grew while in Scandinavia. Now his return to Prague, with its new Provisional Theater, gave him the chance to put into action another idea. He had been aware of the operas of Mikail Glinka, the "father of Russian music," who had used the dramatic nature of opera to tell the story of the Russian people. Glinka's music was filled with the rawness of the Russian spirit, which expressed the joys and pain of the population whose spirit braved the travails of Tsars and harsh governments. Russian villagers loved to tell wild tales based on folklore and legends. They were stories rich in imagination.

He immediately pounced on the idea of a Bohemian opera and within just a handful of years produced *The Bartered Bride*, an opera of great buoyancy and jollity. Magical folk dances dominated the music of the opera. It was a lively musical creation of the Bohemian people.

As Smetana reached his fiftieth year, he took stock of his life. He had held strong political beliefs that had nearly cost him his life. Certainly they had hampered his career. Through it all, he fostered nationalism in his music. To his credit, he had composed several operas that were structured directly from the nationalistic spirit. Then, too, his experiences as an observer of the countryside convinced him that nature itself might be a source of inspiration. In addition, he had made a great study of Bohemian stories. He found them to be rich in pageantry and splendor.

All these he pondered.

One evening while walking along the banks of the River Moldau, a thought began to develop into a musical piece. He thought, "Why not use this river, the greatest river of Bohemia, as the point of inspiration for a great orchestral piece?"

He rushed home to his beloved wife and put into words

his developing thoughts. "Carla, I have an fascinating idea for an orchestra work that will tell the story of Bohemia. It will be based on the great Moldau River."

"The river? I can't imagine."

"First, the Moldau begins as two separate streams that have completely different characters. One is fresh and bubbling, while the other is muddy with a slower current. I have jotted down two musical ideas, each a representation of the two streams."

He demonstrated them on the family piano. She was impressed.

"Good ideas. What will you do then?"

"The two streams flow together, coursing the Bohemian countryside and eventually they create the River Moldau."

"I see," she uttered with growing interest. "Show me, on the piano, what the 'Moldau' theme sounds like."

She was enraptured and said, "I think the melody is so beautiful that it could become the national anthem of our beloved Bohemia."

"Exactly what I was thinking too."

Excitedly, he carried on, "After the 'Moldau' theme, the river moves through thick woods and the sounds of hunting horns are heard. The hunting tunes will quickly identify the nature of the outdoors. To represent the forest, I will create music that expresses the beauty and mystery of the dark woods that cover our countryside."

"All right, Bedrich, I've heard sounds of the river and now hunting sounds, but I don't understand how the piece is distinctly Bohemian."

"Well, I've got that figured out too. After the hunting scenes, I imagine there is a great wedding feast alongside the banks of the River Moldau. Imagine a great gathering of family and friends all dancing and singing. Everyone is in a festive mood. That will be the spirit of the music. I will create music so much like a Bohemian dance that people will believe I have quoted a real folk dance. However, the theme will be all my own. I know the music of our Bohemians because it is truly in my blood."

"Go on. Tell me more," she urged.

"After the wedding feast, envision a moonlit night and in an imaginary setting, nymphs dance on the gentle waves that reflect the shining of the moon. The music will be hushed and quiet. The quietude will also prepare the next section. An entirely new scene, one that will greatly contrast, will unfold. In this passage, the river now flows through the Rapids of St. John. The Moldau has grown to mighty proportions. The great boulders on its river bed and a dramatic drop in elevation creates a wild series of rapids. The music will come forth pounding, driving and riveting. It will go on for several minutes. All of it will be based on the opening musical thoughts, transformed into something fierce."

"How will the piece end?"

"The river flows to the sea as a great and broad waterway, while it moves alongside the historic castle of ancient Bohemian kings. At this point, the Moldau theme, is slowed down to give a feeling of grandiose repose. The music will assume a majestic quality. Finally, the work simply ebbs away and vanishes into the sea far beyond what the eye can see."

"Oh, Bedrich, I am in love with it already. Simply hearing you describe your wonderful ideas inspires me. I am sure that all Bohemians will love it. It will not stop there. I predict that people around the whole world will adore it too. Not only today, but far into the future."

Her predictions came true.

Author's note: Jan Clovicek was a fictitious person.

XVII. Incident at Spillville, Iowa

Jeannette Thurber had been blessed with a large bank account which came to her by way of her marriage to Francis Thurber, a millionaire grocery wholesaler. Her newly-found fortune was matched by a love and devotion to great music. It had been fostered by her father who himself was a Danish violinist who insisted on a strong musical education for his daughter. As a youth, Jeannette attended the prestigious Paris Conservatory, a school she hoped might become a model for an American conservatory.

Antonin Dvorak

Following her schooling in France, she returned to America where she eventually became one of the first major patrons of the arts. Her philanthropic efforts brought about the establishment of the American Opera Company and her funds sponsored the New York debut of the Boston Symphony. However, her most lasting gift to the musical world began with the dream of forming a national conservatory. It was to be a school designed for the finest American music students. Its purpose was to establish an uniquely American school of composition. In 1885, her dream became a reality when she founded the National Conservatory of Music of America in New York City. From its inception, she was determined to have a place where promising composition students could study the indigenous elements of American music. From this, she hoped a wholly American music might someday come forth.

The first seven years of the Conservatory were promising, but she knew her dream could not take full flight until she could find someone who could give the conservatory worldwide significance. She sought to create a school as significant as the Paris Conservatory. In 1892 she enticed Antonin Dvorak, a Bohemian national composer of global fame, to the shores of New York City where he took the helm of the Conservatory. He was a devoted composer of Czech and Bohemian music whose compositions evoked the spirit and legends of his homeland. The decision to leave Eastern Europe for America was not an easy one for him. Mrs. Thurber's enticing offer of an annual salary of $15,000 was what it took to draw him across the Atlantic Ocean.

Dvorak gave the National Conservatory the prestige it needed. His name and gifted administrative skills attracted hundreds of talented music students. Of those, Harry T. Burleigh, a young black man, became a close friend and confidante. Burleigh knew of Dvorak's avid interest in native music and introduced the composer to the spirituals of African-American slaves. It piqued Dvorak's interest. Burleigh's introduction to spirituals would pay off by contributing to one of the greatest works in all of musical history.

The school year of 1892-1893 produced a busy dual track for Dvorak. First, he was committed to building the reputation of the Conservatory. He poured himself into administrating the school's needs. Second, he was intent on composing new music. He desperately sought to capture the spirit of America in his works. He determined that the time spent on the distant shores from his homeland would open new doors and windows he could use in his own writing. The year was also a distressing one for Dvorak as he grew homesick. He desperately missed the country he'd left behind.

In the summer of 1893, he boarded a train and headed westward. He aimed toward Iowa, specifically toward a small town in the northeastern corner of the state called Spillville. It was a tiny community of three-hundred, all of them Czechs. They were his own people. He may have been headed west, but he was also headed toward a homey feeling.

The train ride from New York to Spillville took more than four days and nights. Onward at twenty or twenty-five miles per hour, he passed through New York, Pennsylvania, Ohio, Indiana and then into Chicago, Illinois. The train was filled with passengers from throughout the world heading toward the great Columbian Exhibition, also known as the Chicago World's Fair. It was an exposition of the latest gadgets and inventions in America. It praised the White City, as a certain portion of Chicago was known, because it was illuminated by the electric light. Edison's amazing invention, the light bulb, was now being put into large-scale usage. The world, not only Dvorak, was passing through the great Midwest.

Dvorak didn't bother with Chicago, he headed westward on through the Prairie State and northward along the Mississippi River to Spillville. A magical summer unfolded.

Dvorak's more-than-a-thousand-mile train ride had left him even more in the depths of homesick despair. Each passing mile reminded him of the ever-growing distance between him and his beloved homeland. The industrial state of New York filled with its crowded cities, the green mountains of Pennsylvania, the endless farms of Ohio and Indiana and finally the mesmeric prairies of Illinois only reminded him of how far he was from his Bohemian background. His melancholic misery intensified with each passing state.

Music was his great consolation.

While still in New York, prior to his long train ride, he had begun working on a symphony about America. Burleigh's ideas were taking root. The young man introduced Dvorak to "Swing Low, Sweet Chariot," a spiritual of eternal hope. Its haunting melody gnawed at him. Beside the spiritual, Dvorak sought to understand the music of Native Americans too. "Could these be woven into a symphony?" he wondered.

Spillville was hardly more than a wisp of a town. It was a village of small homes dominated by a rather large Bohemian church fully equipped with an organ. Dvorak's happiest days of his American visit were spent with his new friends there and the many hours he spent every day playing the organ and composing music.

It was July, 1893 when Dvorak was up as early as the rooster and made his way to the church. He carried with him a small stack of J. S. Bach organ pieces and a file of music manuscript papers.

After several productive hours of organ playing and composing, Dvorak's routine was interrupted by Alfred Stelkoven and Ladislav Sulka, two fervent church members. They entered the church to make some routine repairs on a few pews. Dvorak was wearied from a hard morning of work and was happy for the company.

"Good day, my friends. What brings you here?" Dvorak asked.

"My wife complained that she tore her skirt on a sliver of wood in a pew. Ladislav and I are here to make sure it doesn't happen again."

Sulka asked Dvorak about the music he'd been playing on the organ. Dvorak replied, "Oh, I was reviewing some of the final sketches of my new symphony."

"Could we hear some of the music? It would be a lot more enjoyable than fixing the seats."

Dvorak was overjoyed to share his creation.

The poignant opening of the symphony mesmerized both men. As he worked through the first movement, Dvorak explained, "This loud section is like the thunderstorms of Iowa. They appear to come out of nowhere. The rolling hills seem to hide, then almost intensify the severity of the storms. And the wind, it's almost like the devil himself stirs it up. I have never witnessed such wildness. I wanted to capture that in the music"

That produced a quick outburst from Stelkoven. "Oh, you should have been year two years ago. We had a tornado!"

That caught Dvorak's attention. "Tornado? I've heard about them. I understand they occur quite often in the summer here in Iowa. What was it like? We don't have many tornadoes in Prague, near to where I was born."

Sulka explained, "The tornado?! It caused more fury than my wife when I don't empty the chamber pot in the morning. I tell you, it stirred up the cows, flattened the corn, pulled the roof off the barn and scared the kids so bad, they would not come out from under the bed. That's not all, the Missus wanted to go back to Bohemia."

Stelkoven told him he witnessed the twister. He said that even though he lived only a few hundred yards away, his house and barn were fine.

Dvorak shook his head. "Only in America." He paused then asked, "Would you like to hear a little more of the symphony. The second movement is much quieter. I used a spiritual melody called 'Swing Low, Sweet Chariot' as a model."

The men nodded and in a moment were treated to some of the most beautiful music they had ever heard. Sulka mopped a tear from his eye and admitted he missed the homeland he'd left twenty years earlier. He had been enticed to leave Bohemia because of the freedom Americans enjoyed and the promise of one-hundred, sixty acres of free land. He never once, though, lost his love for the land he'd left behind.

Dvorak told them, "As moving as the theme of the second movement is, it will take on a whole new level of emotion as the English horn plays it."

Sulka asked, "What's an English horn? Something like the bellowing bagpipes the Irish play?"

"No, it has nothing to do with England or the British Isles. Just the name given to an instrument quite like the oboe, only longer in size and richer in tone quality. Of all the instruments, I think it is most like the human voice, particularly the hefty alto voice of a woman, or the resonance of the tenor voice of a man."

Suddenly a wild commotion occurred at the front entry. It was Mrs. Sulka and she was not happy! The door flew open. It practically came unbolted from its hinges. "Ladislav, the cows have gotten out of the pasture! How many times have I told you to fix that fence?" Her voice had the rawness of a cold, Iowa winter's wind. "Quit your fooling around here and get back to the farm!"

Dvorak quickly moved to squelch the family squabble and invited her to listen to the lovely second movement theme. She agreed to listen, declaring that was better than going back to washing pots and pans. In moments, she too, was moved to tears. The music helped her recall the intense loneliness of leaving her mother in Eastern Europe, then the emptiness within her heart as she crossed the great Atlantic Ocean and finally the forlorn spirit she endured when arriving in a forsaken land like Iowa. It was a place far removed from the joy of friends and the comforts of her own family. The moving music of Dvorak's theme melted her harsh spirit. She told the small group of her desire to return back to Prague for one last visit. She said the words, "Goin' home. Goin' home. I'm a-goin' home…" seem to emanate from the music. The longing of the music perfectly expressed her lonesome spirit. All the abrasive words she had just spoken to her husband had suddenly dissolved into tenderness.

Mrs. Sulka said, "Now, don't get me wrong, the music doesn't depress me. In fact, its beauty haunts me and expresses my own feelings. I love the music and I thank you for composing it. I think only a Bohemian could have written music of such intensity."

Mr. Sulka said, "I think your symphony should have a name."

Stellkoven responded, "Silly man, symphonies don't have names! They are simply given a number, like 'Symphony No. 5' for the fifth symphony the composer has written."

Dvorak explained, "Usually that is the case, but this symphony deserves a title because this symphony is about something. It is not just a piece of music designed to be heard for art's sake. I am going to call this symphony, 'From the New World.'"

Mrs. Sulka smiled. "'From the New World' I like it. It's just like me, I'd like to be from the new world. That is, far, far away from the new world." With that, she took a playful swing at her husband. Fortunate for him, he was used to such provocations. He ducked and Alfred caught the full force of her blow.

Dvorak's laugh could be heard throughout the tiny community.

Author's note: Ladislav Sulka, his wife and Alfred Stelkoven were fictitious persons.

VIII. Incident at Moscow

Nadezhda von Meck moved to her seat in the balcony with the grace of a gazelle and the silence of a kitten. She also came disguised with a wig and a large hat that fell across her forehead, hiding both her despair and her identity. She had taken great care so that no one would recognize her. She moved specifically to the balcony which was practically empty. Few seats had been taken.

"Good," she thought, "no one to disturb my thoughts or distract me from the beauty of the music."

Peter Ilyich Tchaikovsky

Madam von Meck was a slight women with long narrow fingers and a thin drawn face, very much like her slender waist. Her willowy appearance defied the fact that she had given birth to eighteen children. The eleven children who survived were a handful that required an immense devotion of time and care. Now at age 46, Nadezhda was a grief-stricken widow. Karl, her husband, had suddenly taken ill. Even with Moscow's finest physicians making every attempt to save him, Karl left this world. He also left his wife with a great railroad to run. In fact, he willed her two, a pair of railways that demanded no less than her full attention. His ill-timed departure left her with eleven children, two railroads, large estates, not to mention the education of the seven children still at home. She saw to it that they were all properly schooled. Nadezhda was a women of astonishing means. She was also as durable as leather.

For a few moments this evening, Nadezdha would leave the concerns of family and business behind to attend a performance of the Russian Musical Society. She came with a purpose. As a lover of music, and one who excelled at it even as a child, she had a well-developed ear for musical quality. She knew what she needed this evening and perhaps good fortune might fall her way. With the death of her husband, she sought a composer who could write a worthy funeral march as an expression of her grief.

Her attention tonight was focused on the music of a composer she had heard of. She was not personally familiar with his music, but word in society was that his music was richly melodic. He had a flair for making an orchestra sound as colorful as a parade and as impetuous as the heat of the afternoon sun. It was also touched with a melancholy so dark that its emotions moved some to tears. Critics were sometimes harshly critical of such personal sentiments and a few connoisseurs found his music, well frankly, repugnant. She dismissed their opinions. She would decide for herself. Never one to run from controversy, Nadezda von Meck wanted to hear the music of a man who might reach the depths of passion she was feeling.

Tonight she would be introduced to a work of his, entitled *The Tempest*. It was a work for orchestra and its title suggested passion and power. She listened with great interest and considerable approval.

"Perfect," she thought.

The performance convinced her she had found the composer who could express her sorrows.

The following morning Nadezhda wrote a letter to the composer proposing her request. She desired a funeral march to honor the death of her beloved husband. In addition to her words of personal sorrow, she extended complimentary gestures to the composer. Her words told of her deep admiration for his music. Then she added a tantalizing thought. She suggested that if the elegy met her high standards, possibly an arrangement favorable to both of them might be forthcoming. The letter was sent.

The composer was delighted by the request. He was more than happy to comply. The march was delivered on time which, when first performed, met with the widow's approval. Now it was time for her to move forward with more elaborate plans.

Madam von Meck made her next request. It was to offer a more significant challenge to the composer. She was planning a concert at her estate and was insistent on a series of new pieces for violin and piano. His funeral march had assured her that he was more than capable of the new works. She began her second letter to the composer.

"Dear Mr. Tchaikovsky,

I am a fervent admirer of your music. Your melodies soar to great heights while touching the innermost regions of the heart. Your music has touched upon a room of my heart that I cannot share with others. Your music moves me.

I am prepared to make you a special offer. An offer I trust you shall accept in a spirit of appreciation and devotion. I am a great lover of music and feel a personal responsibility to share my personal wealth with the talents of a composer of your renown.

My offer is this. I shall grant you an annual stipend. It will be large enough to support you in an ample living style. You shall use the time to compose music that flows from your heart. Let it be music that expresses the soul of you, Peter Ilyich Tchaikovsky. Let it be music devoid of the worries posed by the harsh and heartless pen of critics. Let it be music that expresses the soul of our great Russia. May it combine the passions of the peasant with the beauty of luxuriant aristocratic living. Let it flow as you intend.

My offer carries an unusual request. It is a request that must be met or I shall be forced to cut off all funds immediately. The request is this. You and I shall never meet. Our association will be an epistolary one. Letters may flow freely and frequently between us. However, that shall be the full extent of our relationship. I do not seek marriage with you. In fact, the idea of such a union is utterly distasteful to me. Do not interpret that to mean it is you who I dislike. It is marriage itself that gives me discomfort.

I trust you will be willing to accept the annual stipend of 6000 rubles. Since this is twenty times the salary of a minor government official, I believe it will allow you to live comfortably with ample time to pursue your great love of composing.

With admiration,

Madam von Meck"

The letter arrived by post. Tchaikovsky's heart jumped at the name affixed to the envelope. Her magnanimous reputation as a supporter of the arts, and her earlier generous commission, gave his heart reason to leap with excitement.

He read the letter. He sat in disbelief. Again, he read it. Its impact was beginning to dawn on him. This was not an opportunity. It was freedom.

"Strange," he commented to himself, "she refuses to make my acquaintance. Of course, I will accept such a generous offer, but how odd."

He responded in his own letter to her.

"Dear Madam von Meck,

I greeted your letter with untold enthusiasm. Its arrival gave me great happiness, not to mention curiosity.

I read its content with even more delight. You offer me a commodity that goes beyond mere financial support. You give me the gift of time. A day without a flood of appointments and obligations is more precious than gold.

I accept your generous terms. I will keep you abreast of my compositions and concerts which I will share freely with you in the form of letters. I promise volumes that will express who I am. They will articulate the reasons I compose music. They will expose my fears and hopes. They will be filled with words that convey my deep appreciation.

Although my heart wishes to meet you face to face so that I might extend my thanks, I promise to put these gracious words on paper. I commit myself to fulfill the anonymity between us as you have requested.

With ever thanks,

Peter Ilyich Tchaikovsky"

The support began. It continued for thirteen years. She provided regular installments that allowed Tchaikovsky to relinquish his teaching post at the Moscow Conservatory and move to a country home in Maidavano.

The years between 1877 and 1890 witnessed a barrage of correspondence between the two. The years were marked by more than twelve-hundred letters that poured back and forth. Revelations about him were aired.

Tchaikovsky wrote.

"My Dear Madam,

I am absorbed in several projects. These compositions gush with my passions. They bring me joy and pain.

I confess that I am a man possessed of great fears and apprehensions. I am one who is filled with conflicts. I suffer from extreme headaches, surely brought on by my frequent bouts of depression. These bring on tears. Episodes of crying set on without reason. They leave me without consolation. In my soul, I protect a deep secret and a love for alcohol which I fear will harm my body. As you can tell, I am a man torn of conflict.

Most serious are the doubts I have concerning my own music. Though nature has bestowed a gift for inexhaustible melody, I struggle constantly to reign in my ideas. My thoughts are too large for the structure that limits them. They are like too many clothes stuffed in a small drawer. They become wrinkled, unattractive and ill-fitting. Oh, that I might be like the greatest composer of all composers. It is Mozart. His every passion is contained perfectly within the structure of his music. I strive to limit my musical imaginations by the logic of a musical genius like Mozart. Yet to do so would limit my own imaginations. Both my life and my music are filled with strife. Yet I continue on.

Thoughts of your generous and continual gifts are always with me.

With gracious thanks,

Your Peter Ilyich Tchaikovsky"

"Dr. Peter,

I read your letter with consternation. I reread it hoping to find hope, peace and understanding. All elude me.

You and I have much in common. We suffer from the world around us. It is as if we live within a shell seeking solace within ourselves. Are we trapped forever?

Over these several years of correspondence I have concealed a form of affection I have developed for you. This adoration haunts me. Is it you or your music that I find attractive? Your music offers me pleasures unfathomable. My soul is elevated to a higher plane. It blesses me. It rejuvenates my aching heart. It offers solace in a world that is a din of displeasure. Your melodies touch me as if your arms surround me. Embraces of warmth. Hugs of cherished love.

I refuse to succumb to such pleasures. Ours shall be lives of denial. Our affections must not be witnessed. We must remain unseen as a pair. Perhaps the unfulfilled love will bring a degree of restless satisfaction to each of us. Odd as that may be.

With distant admiration,

Your Nadezha,"

Then it happened. The dreaded letter appeared at his post in 1890. It read.

"My Dear Peter Ilyich,

I confess the sorrow that floods my soul. These past years have been an onslaught of contradictions. They have been filled with joy, sorrow, happiness, pain, delight, aching, pleasure and regret. Now, my dear friend, all these will end.

My gifts to you will cease with this letter. Not only is the stipend to end, so, too, is our correspondence. I ask that you kindly destroy the letters that you may have kept. They carry the thoughts of my heart, a discourse of feelings I wish no one to know. I trust you will comply with this request.

I take great pleasure in knowing that my fortune has paved the way for your glorious talent. I think of the many ballets, symphonies, suites, overtures, operas and other countless works that have flowed from your imagination. I know that Moscow and all of Russia today thrills of them. I also sense that the world of tomorrow will be moved to tears, be they joyful or sorrowful, by the fruits of your labors.

My elation is dampened by the illness that is besetting me. Doctors tell me it could be tuberculosis. It has left me with a palsy in my arm. Even with this malady, I refuse to dictate to another the words I feel in my heart for you. This will end our correspondence.

At this time of separation, I trust your esteemed reputation will provide you the necessary funds to live as comfortably as you well deserve.

Taking leave of your life,

I am Nadezhda von Meck"

"My Dear Nadezhda,

The words of your last letter struck me like a locomotive at full steam. A thunderbolt could not have hit harder. Though their impact impales my heart, their meaning has not squelched the admiration and affection I have for you and your generosity.

Over these years, our letters have provided me with

healing, as have my works. I am a man who has felt the blows of critics and audiences. Though shocked by your sudden words, I will press forward.

At the moment I have been commissioned to compose a new ballet. Ivan Vsevolozhsky, Director of the Imperial Theatre, has found a children's story written about a Christmas Eve event involving a Nutcracker. The fable was written by E.T.A. Hoffman some time ago. I have been given no less than a year and a half to have the music ready for performance.

As this is the last of our letters, I stand ready to make a confession. Do you recall the time our eyes landed on each other at a concert? The meeting was an accidental one. It was also a heavy and powerful occurrence. I still feel the red warmth of embarrassment on my face. Did I detect the same discomfort on you? I believe I did. As you are certain to recall, I tipped my hat. You, on the other hand, were a flurry of fumbles, not knowing what to do. Though I expect no answer to my questions, I will carry in my heart our brief encounter. I will also treasure each moment that it passes through my mind, particularly in moments of depression.

Again sincere gratitude,

Your Peter Ilyich Tchaikovsky"

The loss of Madam von Meck's generous annual gifts did not inhibit his work. Her final letter was followed almost immediately by a new commission. It was the assignment that produced his most famous work, the *Nutcracker* ballet.

Tchaikovsky approached composing *Nutcracker* like it was an opera. His lush melodies were written as if they were great arias rung out not by singers but by the orchestra. Even in his unabashed romanticism, Tchaikovsky weaved the tiniest details of the story within the elements of each musical gesture.

The ballet springs from Hoffman's fanciful story of a young girl who was given a nutcracker on the eve of Christmas.

The lifeless creature is brought to life in a dream. Tchaikovsky's music creates fantastic escapades of distant lands and places. The music sweeps from the magical dances of sugar plum fairies to the lighthearted representations of marionettes and culminates in a heavenly waltz of the flowers.

The music gives not a hint of the pessimism he fought while working on his masterpiece. Its sparkling melodies, colorful orchestrations and dance-like qualities exude confidence and hope. Not a shred of bitterness meets the listener. Tchaikovsky viewed the work as autobiographical. He was the nutcracker that was breaking up.

XIX. Incident at La Chat Noir in Paris

The man entered the café as a cat. He came alone. His movements were quiet, stealthy and graceful. Every motion was taken with great caution. He took every provision to avoid calling any attention to himself. The pupils of his eyes danced and darted around the room like a feline attuning itself to the dimness of an ill-lit room.

Though his motions were catlike, his appearance was far from it. The man was short with a stout body that bordered on the pudgy. He had a bulging forehead that stuck out from his thick black hair. His hair was long which he combed over his forehead in hopes of covering the bulges. His dark suit and black hat were fitting attire for a man who exuded only gloominess.

The man had come to the café, the *La Chat Noir*, so that he might hear the piano player. He hoped to make his acquaintance. Together the man and his new friend might engage in a good conversation. Perhaps they might even share some common musical ground.

Claude Debussy

He settled into a chair hoping to hide some of his discomfort. The man was ill at ease. His movements exhibited a number of nervous habits, chief among which was his affinity for tobacco. Being a chain-smoker, he lit a cigarette, then puffed on it incessantly filling the room with foggy images. Through the smoky haze he focused his attention on the music coming from the piano.

The piano player was a slight man who was dressed impeccably. Every article of his clothing was properly fitted and neatly pressed. He seemed overly dressed for such a quaint and of-the-way place as *La Chat Noir*. As a musician, the man was quite comfortable performing at the piano, but he was no virtuoso. He played a music that was simple, pleasant and attractive. It was light, whimsical and displayed artistic restraint. Not only that, the character of the music had a peculiar air to it. Although it was odd, the man found the music to be quite palatable. He could think of only two words to describe such music, perfectly French. He spent the rest of the evening listening with increased pleasure and a growing admiration and affinity for both the pianist and his music.

At the close of the evening, the two men met. The pianist was a lively fellow, quick witted, some would even say funny. He had a clever sense of humor and was always ready with a light-hearted story. The cat-like man drew a sharp contrast to his new friend. While the pianist was cheerful with delicate features, the man's appearance was heavy and dark, casting the image of brooding dismay. The two were as different as a dog and a cat. One looked outward, the other inward. One an optimist, the other a pessimist. Although sharply different, they enjoyed each other's company and a friendship quickly developed. They took pleasure in discovering how much they agreed on things. Particularly, they shared like opinions about music. They adored all things French and strongly disapproved of German music. Above all else, both agreed music must be French in its ideals.

Claude Debussy was the catlike man, Eric Satie the pianist. They bonded into an amicable friendship. Such camaraderie setting on so quickly was quite extraordinary for Debussy. He did not take to others easily. In this case he made an exception. Eric Satie, like Debussy, was a composer. They held similar views on several important issues including music, composition and French ideals. Both were driven by a quest for originality in their music. All these combined to give their relationship an immediacy.

A lively discussion ensued.

"What brings you *to La Chat Noir* tonight?" asked Satie.

Debussy replied, "You, my friend. You brought me here tonight. Others have commented on you and your music. I came to hear for myself."

Satie graciously accepted the kind words, then asked, "Did you come to hear something serious, like a great piano sonata written by one of the Germans?"

Debussy shook his head. "Not at all. Quite the opposite. They say you have a remarkable sense of understatement. You prefer the small and simple, not the big and brash." Raising his voice, he added, "Thank goodness for that!"

"So we share French ideals?" Satie asked half as a question and half as an exclamation.

Debussy nodded. "Indeed I do. The music you played this evening exhibits French tastes." Then he asked, "Tell me. The music, is it yours?"

"It is. Do you approve?"

"More than approve, I find it an inspiration."

"What is it that makes it inspirational?" queried Satie.

"Mostly its French qualities. Your music is clever,

light, airy, even whimsical at times," responded Debussy.

Satie told him, "If you find the music whimsical and humorous, let me tell you the titles of some of my works. I once wrote a piece *Three Pieces in the Form of a Pear.* Another I called *Dehydrated Embroyos.*" Satie's eyes danced around the room for effect, then he leaned forward for dramatic impact and delivered his most outrageous name. "Here is a most clever title: *Pieces to Make You Run Away.* Original, don't you think?"

The title brought a generous smile from Debussy. "My guess is the music would be lighthearted, capricious and fickle. Tell me, have you another title to tickle my fancy?"

"I do. All right. How about *Three Flabby Preludes for a Dog?*"

"Absolutely preposterous! That is simply outlandish. But what do the titles mean?"

"They mean nothing. They are mere suggestions of ridiculousness."

"Oh, but they are clever."

Satie set aside his whimsical self and grew more intense. "I believe that music does not have to be serious, nor does it have to say something important. You agree, no?"

Debussy could see this eccentric, yet humble man, saw things as he did. "Agree? But of course! That is the problem with the music of the German composers. Everything is always serious to them. Their music is somber, severe, staid. I find it dull."

Satie proposed, "We Frenchmen must express our values. Our traditions. Our culture."

Debussy could not have agreed more. "Of matters music, I believe we French composers *must*, and I use the word *must*, rather than *should*, throw off German domination."

Satie added, "By all means. For too many years the Germans have held a tight rein on the development of music. Their music is heavy and thick. I would say stodgy at times. It moves with the charm of a locomotive."

Speaking ever more slowly and with greater conviction, Debussy shared his most intense and dark impressions. "My greatest concern is the German composer Richard Wagner. He is dangerous. He acts like there is but one kind of music. It is German music and he is its king. He is the emperor of all German music, therefore the emperor of all music. That kind of thinking is a threat. I fear where it might lead." Dropping his voice and lowering his emotions, Debussy continued, "While the man has heroic German ideals, I admit with a good deal of reservation, that I admire his music. It is great music. I have even borrowed some of his musical innovations, but I greatly distrust the man."

Satie threw up his hands in frustration. "I see it as you do." With a shrug of his shoulders, he added, "But what am I but a simple Frenchman? It would be impossible for me to "out Wagner" Wagner. I cannot dramatize beyond his dramas. Instead, I commit myself to composing simple music, an expression of a simple man enjoying the simple pleasures of life. Good French food. The taste of good French grapes. The conversation of other Parisians. All these bring me happiness."

Debussy admired a man of such directness and he appreciated Satie's affinity for the simple. Although Debussy agreed with his new friend's philosophies, he himself wanted to create music that was more than daft pieces with witty titles. He was on a quest to create an entirely new kind of music, yet had the gravity to pass the test of time. It was a difficult balancing act. Still, his conversation with Satie was proving to be helpful.

He told Satie, "I am a French musician. I call myself that and I intend to remain loyal to the ideals of our great land."

Their exchange continued on for several minutes. It was lively and heartfelt. Then a silence fell causing a lull in the conversation. It gave Satie a moment to bring up the question that had haunted him for some time.

He asked, "Claude, you won the *Prix de Rome*, the greatest prize in all of music. What was it like to win such an honor?"

Debussy buried his head into his arms. "What a misfortune!"

The comment struck Satie odd. It caught him off guard.

Debussy explained, "For years, I worked hard to secure the prize. I am a slow worker." Then he whispered, "My teachers said I was lazy and they may gave been right. But winning such a prize does not just happen. It takes considerable work and it takes effort." He spoke louder, "The prize meant I would be given the most valuable of all gifts, freedom and time. It also meant I was to spend three years in Italy. That became the problem! My stay there was detestable. I hated the people. I hated the food. I hated the music. There was nothing in Italy I could enjoy. Everyday I longed to return to France, to be home in Paris. The situation grew so bad I gave up the prize, packed my belongings and returned to Paris, well before the three years were up."

Satie could understand such frustrations. "That is remarkable. You have principles. I admire that."

"You know, my friend, the thing that gives me hope is Paris itself. It is the center of the cultured world, alive with artists of all persuasions; painters, poets, musicians, composers all sharing their works and ideas. Paris has become the epicenter of all that happens in the arts."

Satie added, "Artists flock here bringing new ideas."

"Which we need greatly."

Debussy began to express his desire to create a new kind of music. "The past century has produced music that is tiring and boring. It is vacuous and stodgy, overburdened with academic details. It has little life and no vitality. It appeals to the head, but not the beauty of the ear."

Satie expressed, "My friend, that is what our conservatories and universities teach."

That brought an uproarious outburst from Debussy. "Rules! Rules! Our teachers only throw rules at us. Meaningless rules! If art is all rules, how can it express the soul of the individual? Does music have to follow rules?"

Satie asked, "Did you study at the Conservatory?"

"I did. What a waste of time! The professors are stuck in their own ways. They see things only from the past. They discourage original thinking."

Satie agreed and added, "Too much counterpoint, don't you think?" He didn't wait for an answer. "They give us nothing new. They use the music of the Germans to teach us. I am tired of music filled with the taste of sauerkraut. Our music should be like the French language; beautiful, flowing, gently expressive and free of rhythm. Ours is a language of poetry, beauty and love."

Debussy agreed. "I have been greatly impressed by our poets, those who call themselves the Symbolists. They speak in images. Their works are filled with suggestions. They hint, avoiding directness and follow the fluid nature of our language. Why can't music be constructed of such vagueness?"

Satie replied, "There are the painters Monet, Manet, Renoir and the others. They are marvelous painters who suggest rather than portray. These Impressionist painters express many of the same issues as the Symbolist poets. They avoid heroic subjects, like gods, wars, battles of the mortals against the immortals. I tell you, my friend, these subjects are overworked, overdone, and over the top. I say we need freshness. We demand music that is fresh and lively."

Debussy carried Satie's ideas even farther. "We must search for music that is sensitive and beautiful. Since I was boy I sought to create new sounds, with fresh sonorities and novel harmonies. For hours I could sit upon these sonorous sounds taking in their essence as a perfume. Then I changed these harmonies ever so slightly by altering a single pitch, just a step or half step. I succumbed to the beauty of each new sonority. The effects were subtle and sensitive."

Satie certainly agreed, "Subtlety and sensitivity are excellent ideals."

Debussy carried on, "Ah, the beauty of language is in its subtleties. Think of a word. Now consider its synonyms. Try me, Eric. Give me a word, let's consider its subtleties."

"How about 'boat'?"

"All right, 'boat.' Vessel. Ship. Craft. Liner. Sailboat. Dinghy. Rowboat. Yacht. Cruiser. Note the slight nuances in each synonym. Each suggests something slightly different. These are models for composing music. Subtle and suggestive."

They discoursed several more minutes on the nature of music, then Satie turned to a new subject. He brought up the great Paris Exposition of the recent past.

"Tell me, Claude, did you attend the great World's Fair last year?"

"Oh, but of course. You too, no?"

"Certainly I did, along with over 6,000,000 people who rode the train that covered the Exposition. The fair gave us the Eifel Tower. What a magnificent icon of our great city Paris. It will live on for hundreds of years. Was I there? Of course I was there."

Debussy confessed, "The fair opened new worlds to me. I heard a sound I had never heard before. It touched the imaginations of my mind casting a vision of a new kind of music. It has been working in my head for the past year."

Satie was intrigued. "Please tell me if you are willing to share a trade secret."

Debussy nodded. "The sound I heard came from a gamelan orchestra."

Satie smiled. "Yes, I heard it too. I believe it came from the island of Java."

Debussy nodded. "Yes, in the South Pacific. The Asians have created a delicate music that floats and suspends without a touch of harshness or dissonance in their music. I was enamored by the sounds of suspended bamboos, metallophones, xylophones, drums and gongs, which were struck with the force of nothing more than a gentle nudge. The music was like the fluttering of a butterfly, moving in the wind without hurry. It was music suspended in its glory. It was a revelation to me. I must find a way to impose the world of the Orient into our music of the Western world."

Satie could see that his new friend Debussy was entranced by the vision. "Are you working on any particular piece at the time?"

Debussy confessed, "I am working on some sketches for an orchestra work."

"Do you have a title yet?"

"I am calling it *Prelude to the Afternoon of a Faun*."

Immediately Satie was transfixed by the idea. "Ah, that appears to be so elusive, so filled with imagery. Sounds perfectly French to me."

XX. Another Incident in Paris

The three men slipped out of the ballet theater as quickly as they could on the night of May 29, 1913. They left through the stage door hoping to avoid the wrath of the audience. The crowd had become an unruly mob on the edge of frenzy. The three fled in concern for their safety. The back door was their ally.

The trio included a composer, Igor Stravinsky, a choreographer, Vaclav Nijinsky and an impressario, Sergei Diaghilev. They rushed down the streets of Paris in a highly agitated state. The darkness of night gave them cover, for which they were thankful. To any observer, their quick pace and animated conversation indicated something was seriously wrong. It was. Stravinsky, the one with large glasses, a small head and mustache was obviously the most disturbed. He was in fact, nigh unto tears. Distraught was written all across his face. The three were headed to a restaurant for food, conversation and most of all, for refuge. They needed a place to escape the turmoil they had just witnessed. For that matter, it was turmoil they themselves had created.

Igor Stravinsky

They arrived at a café and found a table in a dark corner positioned far away from the entrance. They wanted to be alone. They kept a wary eye open for disgruntled customers who might have attended the ballet. Of the three, Stravinksy was the most dejected. As he reached the table, he broke down in sobs. He was heartbroken. The night had not turned out as he had expected.

Between sobs he said, "I had an idea that the night would bring a scandal."

Diaghilev exclaimed, "A scandal? You enticed a riot!"

Nijinsky confessed, "I knew my novel approach to choreography would cause chaos and skepticism."

Diaghilev laughed. "Skepticism? What I heard were boos and hisses. I have never experienced anything like it."

Stravinsky shook his head in deep dismay. "The ballet was a disaster. The night was a disaster. Worse yet, I am a disaster."

Nijinsky felt the same way about himself. "You and I. Two disasters!"

To describe the night as a disaster was a vast understatement. It was a night that shook the art world forever. Both dancing and music were rocked to their foundations. Never before, and never again, would such a reaction be provoked from an audience of concert goers. It made heroes and revolutionaries out of all three.

Igor Stravinsky came to that performance as a relatively little-known Russian composer. His fame rested on several short orchestra works and two impressive ballets. His reputation was limited to Paris and Russia. That night changed him forever. Nijinsky had built a fabulous career as a ballet dancer. On this occasion, he had assumed a new role, he was the choreographer. Instead of dancing, he designed all the movements for the dancers. These two extraordinary talents were brought together by Diaghilev, the potent leader of the Russian Ballet Company.

At the restaurant, Stravinsky and Nijinsky were caught in the sullen depths of despair. Diaghilev was not. Tonight, he saw fame and fortune. He broke the gloomy atmosphere with a loud laugh and said, "Don't you see what has happened tonight? Think of the publicity we created tonight. We could not have paid money for the incredible press reports we will get."

Of the three, he was the only one who understood the importance of the reaction of the crowd. While the other two were licking their wounds, Diaghilev was offering hope, something Stravinksy and Nijinsky needed desperately at this hour.

Only a few hours earlier, the evening began in high hopes. It ended in dashing despair. The three had collaborated on a new ballet, the *Rite of Spring*. This was the night of the premiere. The ballet was all theirs. They created it, produced it and now were reviewing it. It was a ballet that caused a riot.

How could a ballet prompt a crowd to riotous behavior? First, it had a provocative title. *Rite of Spring* suggested something horribly barbaric. Second, it was violent, harsh, rough and discordant, quite a contrast from the elegance, charm, grace and beauty expected from ballet. Third, its storyline was pagan. The story centered around the sacrificial death of a young maiden whose life was surrendered to nature. A dance of sacrifice was heresy to Christian teachings. At its core, *Rite of Spring* was corrupt and pagan. Controversy was inevitable.

The tale came as a vision to Stravinsky several years earlier. In 1910, he described the idea to Diaghilev, a man who understood the composer's enormous talents and his desires for intrigue and controversy.

Stravinsky explained to Diaghilev, "I had a fleeting vision. I saw in my imagination a solemn pagan rite. There were wise elders all seated in a circle. They watched as a young girl danced herself to death. They were sacrificing her to satisfy the god of spring." Then he revealed his plan. "This is the vision I am contemplating for a ballet."

"A sacrificial dance for a ballet?" thought Diaghilev. The idea ricocheted through his mind bringing about wild images. He could see the publicity and profit to gain by such an outrageous idea. A pagan rite as the basis for a story of ballet. The two ideas stemmed from worlds drastically apart.

"How long would it take to compose such a ballet?" he eagerly asked.

Stravinsky thought. "I should imagine a year. Of course, that would be only the notes. There would have to be a lengthy time of preparation, of imagination, of conceptualizing such a fantastic production."

Diaghilev had always been impressed by the young composer's rich mind. He saw greatness in his music. "Igor, you are a genius. On many occasions, I have told people that you are to be watched. You are destined to be famous. This *Rite of Spring* could be the ballet that will place your name into history." He stopped to ask, "Are you prepared to begin work on it immediately?"

Stravinsky was not. "I need to compose another ballet before I attempt the *Rite of Spring.*"

"Is that so? Just what do you have in mind?"

"I have a clever idea for a plot. It is the story of a puppet who comes to life. I promise it will revolutionize music by its innovations. The title *Petrushka* is even more clever."

"Petrushka?"

"Yes, it is the puppet's name."

"Just what kind of innovations do you have in mind?"

"I have been experimenting with combining two separate key signatures played at the same time."

"Two different key signatures played at the same time? Preposterous! Doesn't that destroy the music?"

"I don't know if it is preposterous, but it certainly is revolutionary. I intend to combine the keys of C Major and F# Major at the same time. Is that revolutionary enough?"

Diaghilev could not imagine two different keys competing with each other at the same time. It would be like war. Two great armies pitted against each other.

"Igor, if I didn't trust you so, I would say your idea is ludicrous. However, your great ballet *Firebird* proved you are capable of cleverness. Go ahead, Igor, compose *Petrushka*. I will see to it that it is performed. Then we can discuss this pagan ballet, the *Rite of Spring*."

Stravinsky was appreciative. "Thank you, Sergei, I owe my entire career to you."

"No, my friend, you are a genius. It is my job to support great artists who create spectacular art. We owe our careers to each other. Remember, we are all Russians. We stick together as a team!"

Sergei Diaghilev was a powerful man who could make things happen. When he first heard Stravinsky's music, he was drawn to its power, imagination and originality. A partnership was formed. In the course of four years, the team completed and performed three magnificent ballets. It was an association that would rock the world of ballet and music.

Although they were Russians, their ideas and creations needed a city eager for new and innovative material. They headed for Paris. It was a modern city filled with artists, poets, composers, craftsmen and free thinkers of all persuasions. As a cosmopolitan city with an open mind, Paris offered them all the components they needed for success.

Stravinsky began work on the *Rite of Spring* in Switzerland, his adopted home. He rented a room not much larger than a closet. As a thinker, he was original. As a worker, he was methodical, habitual and painstaking. He was also a musical explorer and experimenter: Christopher Columbus and Louis Pasteur rolled into one. Each morning and afternoon he sat at an upright piano pounding out harsh, dissonant chords. It drove the lady downstairs crazy.

Marianna, the apartment caretaker, shook her head. "All day long he plays wrong notes on the piano."

Her friend Francine was fascinated. "What does he plan to do with all these wrong notes?"

"He says he is composing a ballet."

"He is a composer?"

"Not just a composer. A famous composer."

"How can he be famous if I have never heard of him?"

"They *say* he is famous. Whether he is famous or not, he is composing a ballet filled with wrong notes."

"How do you know they are wrong?"

"I know what sounds right or wrong. Everything he composes sounds wrong!"

"The whole thing sounds insane. A ballet of wrong notes? That can't be. Ballet is graceful and filled with beauty. Are you sure he is writing a ballet?"

"Of, but of course." Then she added in a whisper,

"Yesterday, I found an inscription carved into the piano."

"What did it say?"

"I don't know if I understand what this means. The carving read, 'Here I am composing the *Rite of Spring.*' What does that mean? The *Rite of Spring?*"

"With all those wrong notes, maybe he should call it the 'Wrong of Spring.' Actually, 'Rite of Spring' sounds like a disgusting pagan thing. That's what it means. I can't imagine that something so earthy as a dance to the death to be fit for a ballet."

Marianna picked up a broom and made a few sweeping gestures. She stopped, then said, "There is something else that drives me batty. It is his constant loud pounding and the reckless stamping of his foot. Bang. Bang. Bang. Nothing is regular either. I cannot feel a steady beat."

"You say it is a ballet and the rhythms are irregular? How can he be writing a ballet that has no consistent beat?"

Marianna left the room muttering, "A sacrificial dance. Pounding and irregular rhythms. A melody I cannot discern for the life of me. And wrong notes. Now, I ask you, is that the making of a ballet?"

As the days approached for the premiere, it was time to combine music and dance. Stravinsky and Nijinsky could be seen together frequently. Their discussions often became heated with the composer pounding out the music at the piano and the choreographer shaking his head. They often clashed.

Being the composer, Stravinsky had the upper hand. Any ballet begins with the music. The choreographer is left to interpret the music as a continuum of movement and motion. It required a thorough understanding of the music. Stravinsky's music was entirely new, unlike anything heard before. First, Nijinsky had to grind the music into his head, devise the movements for each dancer, then teach the dancers the interpretation. The newness of the music and its radical nature drove the choreographer to aggravation. Matters were not helped as Stravinsky felt it was his duty to teach Nijinsky the basics of music theory.

"Igor, I do not need a lesson in music theory. I need to hear the music you wrote. That is why I am here."

Stravinsky paid him practically no attention. "In traditional composition, the downbeat receives the strongest impulse. That is the natural impulse of the music."

Nijinsky could not have cared less. "I don't care what rules Beethoven, Bach or any other Russian for that matter, follows. I simply must hear the music you have written."

Stravinsky played a few more bars, Nijinsky choreographed them.

"Wrong, your rhythm is all wrong!" Stravinsky screamed. "You are not feeling the music. The accents normally fall on the downbeats of each measure. Certainly you understand that."

"Normally they do! But your music is not normal! You have given me nothing to feel the downbeat."

"This is primitive music. It is inspired by the pagans who have no educated knowledge of written music."

"The music may be primitive, but my dancers are skilled and learned artists. I must give them something they can understand."

Stravinsky came up with a suggestion. It landed flat as a prairie farm. "In the *Firebird* ballet, we had the dancers say Ser-Gei Dia-ghi-Lev. Five syllables. Five beats. One syllable for each beat."

"Yes, but your music was consistently in a meter of five. This ballet is a mixture of all sorts of meters. How can the dancers dance if they cannot feel a regular meter?"

The arguments continued for days. In frustration, Nijinsky decided to forget the music, and create dance movements that corresponded to the basic feel of the music. They would have to learn the steps by rote, forget listening to the music.

Then the orchestra rehearsals began. The reactions of the musicians were not nearly as severe as the dancers. However, they had never witnessed such complex, harsh, or testy music as the *Rite of Spring*. The opening bassoon passage was next to impossible to play. The tunings, awkward fingerings and the odd sonority gave the bassoonist fits. Conducting the score required all-new baton techniques. The constant changing of meters presented horrific problems for conveying downbeats or cueing the correct players. The musicians were free and open in their criticisms. Yet through it all, they understood they were on the cusp of something new and different. That helped alleviate some of their apprehensions.

Finally opening night came. The evening began quietly. The strange bassoon solo at the outset began to create consternation within the audience. Even a few composers in the crowd were puzzled by the sound. What instrument was playing that passage? The music was eerie, mysterious, strange. It evoked a few catcalls from the audience. From there, the music grew intense. It was rough-edged. A series of pounding, harsh chords (those wrong-note chords Lady Marianna had criticized) and thick sonorities were driven with jack-hammer intensity. They were echoed by hard drumming from the timpani. The French horns combined with the violins to produce a series of percussive explosions. The audience grew hostile. Shouts of "cacophony" were hollered out. A chorus of boos and hisses followed by loud whistles and catcalls began to drown out the music. Dancers could not hear the music. The crowd was angry. What was happening to the lovely form of ballet, or the beauty of music? What they were hearing was ugly and disastrous. In an uproar people stomped from their seats in anger, disgust, frustration. The manager of the house tried to maintain order by flashing the lights off and on. In vain, Nijinsky screamed out directions to the dancers who could not hear the music because of the roar.

Meanwhile, a second group was forming. They welcomed the new music. They assumed an entirely different position. It was led by French composer Maurice Ravel who was crying "Genius! Genius!" Two hostile camps formed. Pandemonium began to break out. Worse yet, the place erupted into fisticuffs. An open brawl ensued. Panic hit Stravinsky. In a rush, he slipped from his seat, moved backstage, with his emotions ripped apart by the outbreak. Stravinsky, Nijinsky and Diaghilev escaped from what now had become a full-scale riot. The left in fear of their lives.

The date was 1913, just thirteen years into the twentieth century. It also marked the passing off of the old art. A new day in music had dawned. Then again, the world was changing. Within a year of that fateful May night, the entire Western World was engulfed in the "war to end all wars."

The *Rite of Spring* was a harbinger that suggested the world would never be the same. It also made Igor Stravinsky the musical giant of the twentieth century.

Author's note: Marianna and Francine were fictitious persons.